Thelon

A River Sanctuary

David F. Pelly

Thelon

A River Sanctuary

Copyright © 1996 By David F. Pelly

Main entry under title:
Thelon - A River Sanctuary
Includes bibliography references and index.
ISBN 1-895465-21-4

1. Thelon River Valley (N.W.T.) - History.
2. Thelon Game Sanctuary (N.W.T.).
3. Canoes and canoeing – Northwest Territories – Thelon River.
F1100.T54P45 1996

I. Canadian Recreational Canoeing Association.
II. Title.
FC4195.T54P45 1996   971.9'4   C95-920804-6

Publisher:

CANADIAN RECREATIONAL CANOEING ASSOCIATION

1029 Hyde Park Rd., Suite 5, Hyde Park, Ontario Canada N0M 1Z0
Phone (519) 473-2109/641-1261 Fax (519) 473-6560
new address September 1996:
P.O. Box 5000, 446 Main St. West, Merrickville, Ontario Canada K0G 1N0
Call directory assistance at (613) 555-1212 for our new telephone number as of September 1, 1996.

The author wishes to acknowledge the assistance of the Canada Council during the research and writing of this book as well as the support of Canadian Airlines International and Canadian North.

Canadi∍n   Canadi∍n *NORTH*

Other books by the Author:
Expedition – An Arctic Journey Through History on George Back's River
Qikaaluktut – Images of Inuit Life (Illustrated by Ruth Annaquusi Tulurialik)
Inuit of the North
The Kazan – Journey into an Emerging Land (eds. with Chris Hanks)
Cover Photo: David F. Pelly, inset: Laurie M. Pelly

For my parents, JFP & JKP,
who first put me in a canoe,
who fostered my urge to seek
the wilderness, and who,
in their 70th year, paddled
this river sanctuary with me.

contents

Maps

Preface

What is wilderness? Is it both a physical place and a concept, or perhaps an attitude? The very word conjures up a sense of remote mystery.

For me, the Thelon is the quintessential "wilderness." But what is wilderness for me may not be to the next fellow, particularly if that fellow's grandfathers lived in my wilderness, and hunted there for their food, as did both Dene and Inuit before white man ever thought about the Thelon. And yet we agree, really: it is a region where industrialized society's impact is minimal, where nature remains the supreme force. It is a place where a human presence is only incidental, and where mystery prevails. Such is the Thelon valley, still today.

This book aims to tell you the Thelon's story, a tale replete with adventure, intrigue, joy, sorrow and drama. I'm not going to harp on the Thelon wilderness being the largest, the wildest, or the greatest — though it may be any of those in Canada, or in North America, or in the world? — but it does in some way stand apart. In the Canadian context, it was recognized as a valuable wilderness, as a sanctuary, very early. Canada as a dominion was only 60 years old when the Thelon Game Sanctuary was created by Order in Council. That gives it seniority, as formally recognized wilderness, which exceeds most (if not all) others in this country.

But wilderness, to survive as wilderness, needs a voice. Its own voice cannot be heard beyond those who enter it as a sanctum. It cannot speak for itself, to defend itself against our intrusions. That underlies my motive for writing this book: to add my effort to the communal voice speaking on behalf of the Thelon wilderness.

That voice includes many others, to be sure, each of whom knows parts of the Thelon valley or parts of its history much better than I do. Whenever possible I have conferred with them; I was privileged to meet and listen to several old Thelon hands. I am indebted to numerous people who co-operated with my efforts to compile the Thelon's story: they know who they are, and to them I convey my sincerest thanks, literally from coast to coast to coast in Canada and overseas in Europe. I cast my net as widely as possible.

It is the richness of human experience, layered on top of the natural splendour of the river valley and its wildlife, that really sets the Thelon apart. The place has a history, both Native and non-Native, which gives it standing beyond the intrinsic value of wilderness itself. That may prove to be the difference between preservation and destruction of the Thelon wilderness; history may be its saving grace. This book is my attempt to render that history accessible, thinking it may make a difference to the future. The Thelon is a wilderness which deserves a voice and, I believe you'll agree, it offers a Canadian tale that ought to be told.

I am confident of that because I have been there, I have experienced the Thelon's mystery — a mystery which this book explores but could not possibly explain.

I'm well aware that I am not an old-timer in the Thelon. I first travelled there in mid-winter 1984 with a small party of Inuit hunters from Baker Lake, up the river valley nearly to (but not over) the eastern boundary of the game sanctuary. It captured my imagination then and I've been back several times since: on canoe trips in summer, and in winter with my friends Tulurialik, Mannik and Piryuaq.

Over the years, the Thelon wilderness has become a special place for me, bestowing lasting gifts and memories. Although this book as a whole is my spiritual response to the place, most of my personal experience of the Thelon is not to be found in these pages. I could describe meeting Laurie on the Thelon: I was there researching a story on assignment for an American canoeing magazine; she was there on a package holiday, her first wilderness canoe trip, with other Americans as diverse as a midwestern farm-wife, a sci-fi writer from California exploring "a parallel universe," and a security guard from JFK airport seeking to escape "the electromagnetic radiation" in New York. Together Laurie and I have returned to the Thelon several times, to paddle various parts of the watershed, and when we're not up there, we're often talking about the place; it remains central to our life, and her multi-dimensional support as I worked on this book has been unfailing. I could tell you about the grizzly that swam across the river and stalked along the bank toward our camp ... or the grinding portages enduring shirt-soaking heat and swarming bugs ... or sitting quietly atop an esker looking out over thousands of square miles of rolling tundra ... or surveying geese and falcon and musk-ox populations in the aid of science ... or paddling across wave-tossed lakes into relentless headwinds ... or the terror of facing a charging musk-ox ... or the beauty of the midnight light ... or being blockaded, first by ice then by gale-force winds, on the big lakes — all of which have happened. But that is my story, best saved for a campfire circle some day, and this is the Thelon's story.

I offer it — imbued with respect, admiration and gratitude for all the old-timers, both Native and non-Native, who have gone before — in the hope that this small voice recounting their stories, the Thelon's story, will serve to buttress its defenses and enhance its chances of survival as a wilderness. It is, after all, part of us.

D.F.P.

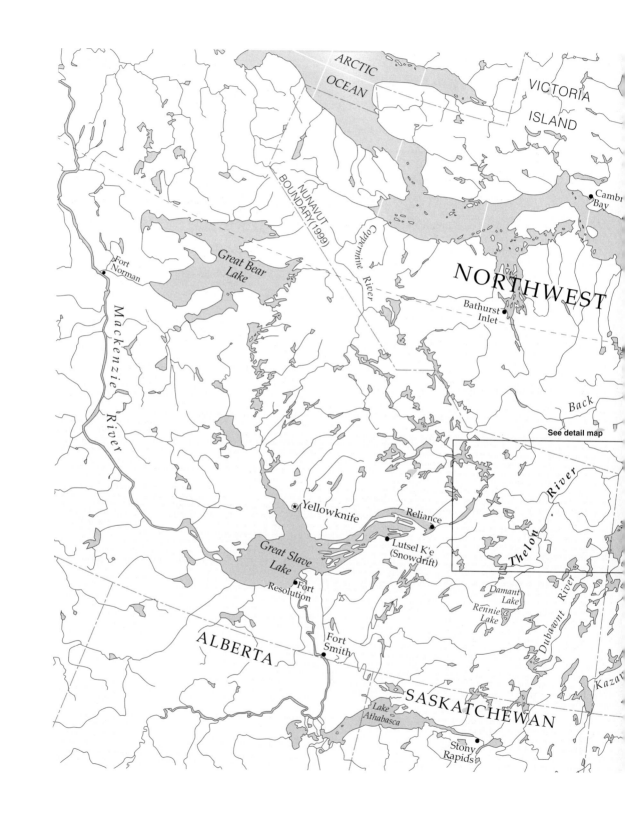

ARCTIC
OCEAN

VICTORIA
ISLAND

Cambr
Bay

NUNAVUT
BOUNDARY (1999)

Fort
Norman

Great Bear
Lake

Coppermine River

NORTHWEST

Bathurst
Inlet

Mackenzie River

Back

See detail map

Thelon River

⊛ Yellowknife

Reliance

Lutsel K'e
(Snowdrift)

Great Slave
Lake

Dubaant River

Fort
Resolution

Damant
Lake

Rennie
Lake

ALBERTA

Fort
Smith

Kazan

SASKATCHEWAN

Lake
Athabasca

Stony
Rapids

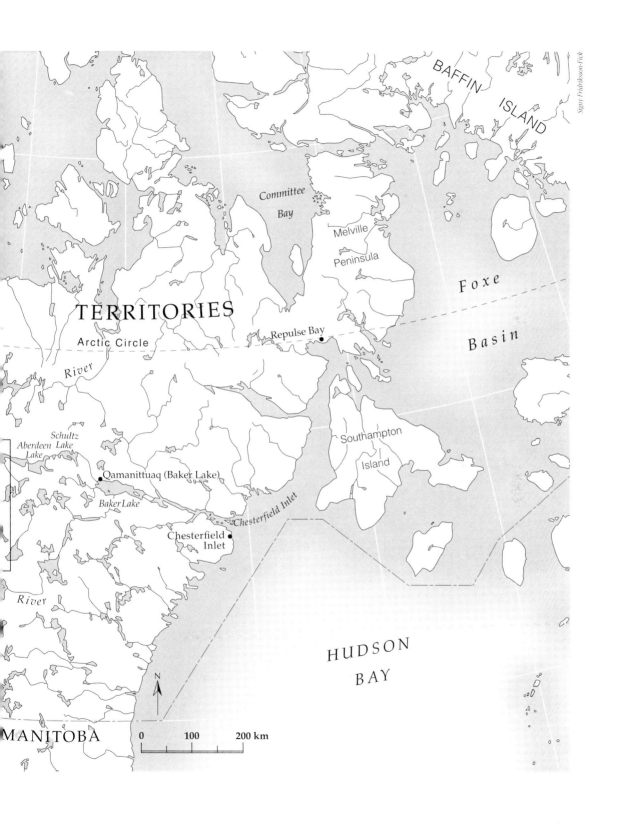

BAFFIN ISLAND

Committee Bay

Melville Peninsula

Foxe

Basin

TERRITORIES

Arctic Circle

Repulse Bay

River

Southampton Island

Schultz Lake
Aberdeen Lake

Qamanittuaq (Baker Lake)

Baker Lake

Chesterfield Inlet

Chesterfield Inlet

River

HUDSON BAY

MANITOBA

N

0   100   200 km

Signy Fridriksson-Fick

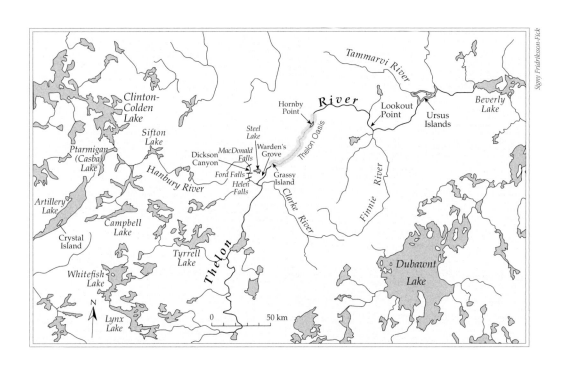

Clinton-Colden Lake

Sifton Lake

Ptarmigan (Casba) Lake

Hanbury River

Artillery Lake

Crystal Island

Campbell Lake

Tyrrell Lake

Whitefish Lake

Lynx Lake

Thelon

Steel Lake

Dickson Canyon

MacDonald Falls

Ford Falls

Helen Falls

Warden's Grove

Grassy Island

Hornby Point

River

Thelon Oasis

Clarke River

Finnie River

Tammarvi River

Lookout Point

Ursus Islands

Beverly Lake

Dubawnt Lake

N

0   50 km

1

Enter the Sanctum

Free again. The first, fleeting moments alone beside a barrenlands river deliver a sensation I can never forget. Impossible to hold onto, it is nonetheless so profound that its memory is permanent. Left alone beside the river, with no more than a tiny pile of gear, a silent travelling companion, and an immense wilderness all around, the solitude penetrates through every sense, every pore of my body. It is palpable, flowing over me like a wave.

I have been here before, indeed to this very spot beside the Thelon River, but more important, to this emotional moment at the beginning of a barrenlands canoe trip. It is familiar, and expected, and all the more profound because of that. There is mystery, but the feeling must have something to do with the anticipation of what lies ahead, of what the wilderness holds in store. One thing is certain: we have escaped from the impositions of "civilized" life, though it is temporary, and somewhat contrived to be sure. But nothing could be more real than the river at my feet, with its crystal clear water, or the expanse of wilderness beyond its banks, or our deep impression of isolation. We look at each other; the sight of just a single person in this vast landscape only emphasizes our solitude. There is a feeling of having awoken from a dream, to find yourself within a beautiful, peaceful sanctum. There is stimulation everywhere, and yet there is nothing, absolutely nothing, imposing itself upon you.

The closest human settlement is about 450 kilometres away. In fact, the Northwest Territories capital Yellowknife to the west, the Inuit community of Qamanittuaq (Baker Lake) to the east, Stony Rapids in northern Saskatchewan to the south, and Bathurst Inlet on the arctic coast to the north are all roughly equidistant from our position in the middle of continental North America's largest tract of wilderness. In the Twin Otter that brought us here, any one of the four settlements could be reached in about three hours. By canoe, now our only choice, we could also head toward any of the four destinations — such is the extensive network of waterways that weaves together the patterned landscape of the northern wilderness. But even the most direct route, downstream to Baker Lake, will require nearly a month of paddling. We have allowed 40 days.

Before anything else, we are both eager to walk up onto the land. We breathe in the unique aroma of crushed tundra plants and lichens, as our first footsteps carry us up the slope. In minutes we are high enough above the river to look up and down its course, detached from the immediate sense of its current that absorbed us at the water's edge. Now we see its full breadth, a hundred and fifty, maybe two hundred metres across. The water shines blue and silver, as clean as any water on Earth can be. This river will run through the centre of our lives for the rest of this summer. It is like an old friend, I think, and smile.

Just downstream beyond the bend where the river disappears there is, I know, a cliff-face housing a colony of swallows in their beehive-like nests. We will visit them in the days ahead. Upstream, there is a regularly used peregrine falcon nest that I want to check. But there is no rush. First we will make camp here, where the plane has deposited us — as much by chance as by choice — and spend a day or two adjusting to the river valley's cycle of life. We are here to become a part of this valley, as much as that is humanly possible. And that means first we must find the rhythm.

So we go for a walk. The top of the closest rise will do just fine for now. Other, higher, more distant hills can wait for tomorrow or the next day. For now we want simply to let the wilderness wrap its arms around us, embrace us if it will. As we walk, the land spreads out before us, mile after mile after mile of open tundra. There are shades of green that defy description. Here and there, the land sprouts boulders, as if exposing a dry river course; in fact it is the signature of some ancient glacial action. In places we walk over the exposed granite surface of the Canadian Shield, scraped clean by the Ice Age glaciers, which gouged striations into the 2.5 billion-year-old rock at our feet. It is the oldest rock in the world, I remind myself, looking up again into the distance. Pockets of spruce dot the landscape to the east, for we are near the edge of the Thelon Oasis. Trees grow here, several hundred kilometres north of the treeline, in the shelter of the river valley. Beyond the valley, north and south, is the treeless barrenlands. In all that space, as we search to the horizon, there is not another human being. There are other animals, to be sure, but we can see no movement, apart from the occasional pair of Harris' sparrows hopping nervously from boulder to boulder as we pass through their territory.

Off in the distance we see a ridge of golden sand, winding snake-like across the land. An esker, it marks the course of a glacial river during the latter stages of the last ice age, which retreated from here between eight and nine thousand years ago, leaving this valley flooded by a post-glacial lake. It took centuries, but eventually nature created this panorama of life, with all its subtle hues.

As glacial Lake Thelon drained, the climate warmed, and vegetation spread over the newly exposed surface. It was not long before small mammals moved north from the refuges sought during the ice age. Then came the caribou, and shortly after, Man followed.[*]

The land may *seem* empty today as we stand high above the river and absorb its grandeur, but the humbling reality is inescapable. There is life everywhere around us, and there has, in the past, been human life in this scene. Native people before us were here for thousands of years, living on this land and from its wealth. The mysterious signs of their presence are there, and in the days ahead we will look closely to see them.

Now it is time to return to the riverbank, retrieve our pile of gear, and set up camp. There is no urgency. The huge, open sky is clear of cloud. The weather promises to be agreeable for awhile. The sun is still high enough in the western sky to suggest that it may not set tonight. It is early July, when daylight persists around the clock.

The first day of a barrenlands canoe trip is always full of adjustments, a time for the realignment of thought. It starts dramatically with the roar of turbines as the Twin Otter lifts off, followed by the traditional salutory waggle of the wing tips and then, moments later, silence and solitude. For me, there is a sense of homecoming.

———◆———

Later, the tent up, the gear sorted, and supper cooked, we celebrate our arrival. In the tradition of voyageurs and Native travellers everywhere, we offer a small amount of a treasured commodity to the river and to the land. I splash some of our scant supply of rum into the river. It must be enough to feel the sacrifice, "to please the river-gods." Our routine for the next 40 days will unfold at the whim of the river. Life now is a simple matrix of food, shelter, travel, and the land — and *the river runs through it*.

That night, as we settle into our sleeping bags, the sun shines into the tent through the north-facing bug-screen door. I glance at my partner writing in her daily journal. "Home again!" she has penned boldly in her first entry for the summer. I smile inside, content to know that she too feels that way. It will be a good summer on the Thelon.

———◆———

* See Appendix IX: A Short Geological History of the Thelon Valley.

My paddle dips into the bright clear water of the Thelon and silently urges our canoe forward, stroke upon stroke, in a rhythm as gentle as the current's flow. By now, after several days, it almost feels like *our* river. My eyes cast upward onto the land, and the daily feast begins. It is, I cannot help but remark, such beautiful country. I feel privileged to be here, like a visitor to a holy sanctum, a place I could never possess.

Why am I here? The question haunts me, even though on the surface the answer seems obvious. But why *here*? What is it about this place that draws me and many others back time and again on modern-day canoe trips? What is it about this place that nourished the lives of those before us, not only physically but spiritually? What is about this place that moved the barrenland trappers to call it "The Country?" What is about this place that made it really the last frontier in continental North America, a place where explorers, map-makers, and scientists only came in the course of this century? What is it about this place? Why, now, am I *here*?

My canoe drifts forward and the mystery begins to unfold, subtly, in the way of this wilderness sanctuary. For me, something about this place speaks of rebirth; why, I am not certain. It has become an essential part of my existence. I am here to answer a need, to seek something inside — inside me, inside humanity, inside this place. This river valley offers the inner sanctum of my quest where, surely, the answers can be found.

We are in the heart of the so-called Thelon Oasis, that stretch of the river valley from the Hanbury junction down to just below Hornby Point. The spruce grow thickly here, defiantly holding their position well north of the treeline. The banks on either side of the river are dense enough with spruce that a fleeing wolf or caribou or moose can disappear in an instant. Nevertheless, looking up higher, to the hills on either side that form this valley, one can see the tundra landscape that belongs to this latitude. It is only in the low-lying portion of the valley that the forest remains so thick, in places almost impenetrable.

Four to five thousand years ago, the entire area, even the hills, was heavily treed. While walking up in the hills, I have come upon old stumps as big as my thigh where there is nary a live tree to be seen. The forest coverage that far north was temporary; in due course it retreated south. Today trees survive only down close to the river. The valley is oriented in such a way that these trees are sheltered from the worst blast of the arctic climate. The soil is relatively rich. The river itself rises from the southwest, so its warmer water nurtures the Oasis. Conditions, so far, have conspired against the arctic environment to sustain this small pocket of forest growth.

It takes only a few days to transit the Oasis by canoe, and even here a tongue of tundra landscape occasionally licks down to the river's edge, enough to remind you where you really are, in the barrenlands. It is seldom more than a fifteen minute walk away from the river to the forest's outer edge, as the land climbs away from the water. There, I can stand on the open tundra.

All of these mysterious elements of the land surround me as our canoe moves forward with the river's current. Details that sometimes I do not even see. Together they comprise the wilderness that embraces the passer-by. Together they have a power and influence that none could achieve on its own. Assembled into the landscape of the Thelon valley, from its sweeping grandeur to its detailed ground patterns, it is enough to humble the transient human. Always as I paddle, I allow ample time for walking, for leaving the canoe on the beach and climbing up into the hills. That is where this valley offers its greatest gifts.

Nevertheless, the river itself holds a compelling fascination. The Thelon River drains a vast area, approximately 150,000 square kilometres. The result is that even here in the Oasis, where the land is quite flat, the water flows with a noticeable current, inexorably toward the sea, still 1,000 kilometres away. In the early summer, shortly after break-up, the river is fairly flying, with a peak discharge that exceeds 4,000 cubic metres per second. Usually sometime in early June, the ice can no longer contain the pressure of the underlying water, swollen by the melting snow. So it bursts, and great chunks of ice go hurtling down the river. Only by July 1 can one usually count on finding an ice-free river, and then only as far downstream as Beverly Lake. The large lakes between there and the sea often remain partially covered by floating ice until the end of July, sometimes even into August.

Beside the river just upstream from Beverly Lake there is a small cabin used by the Water Survey of Canada crews as they do their rounds of the northern rivers, measuring water levels and discharge. In the cabin's log-book, in 1991, one member of the crew made the following entries. They illustrate the drama of spring break-up.

June 8 - all bench marks underwater, river at door step ... total discharge 9135 cubic metres per second or 322,647 cubic feet per second ... She's really boogieing — that's equal [in volume] *to 80 semi-trailers per second rolling down the river.*

June 28 - water has dropped some 6 metres since June 8th. An historic year on the Thelon. We have probably witnessed a 1 in 100 year flood.

The river now is running more slowly, but still it is running, carrying our canoe — and us — through the valley. It is the river that binds together all these thoughts and all these sights. It is running day and night, but it is more than a constant flow. For us, the travellers, as for all the other living things that inhabit the valley, the river is the source of life. It reflects the life around it even as it sustains that life.

I look down into the water, into the river, past its glassy surface. Every square inch of that surface is forever changing. But beyond it is the constant heart of this valley. It is linked to every event, to every thing within the valley. Even the most desolate craggy rockface becomes a fluid part of the landscape because it lies beside the river. The river's surface separates the component parts: this bank from that, land from sky; and just as suredly it ties them together, just as it joins into one all the tiny tributaries and rivulets that spill down its banks. All of this affords the river a tremendous sense of power, a power even greater than its annual break-up flood. In the end, the river joins all the barren landscape through which it flows into a single unity, and connects it to the sea, and thus to the rest of the world. It is, after all, our river, our sanctum.

2

The-lew-dezeth

Three hundred years ago, the valley of the Thelon River looked much as it does today. There is one important difference: it was utterly unknown to white man. No European had ventured so far into the interior of North America. The closest outpost of the British traders was at York Factory beside the mouth of the Nelson River on Hudson Bay, established in the 1680s. There the British had developed communication and trade with the nearby Cree, but they dreamed of greater wealth to be found farther afield to the northwest.

The Cree spoke of far-off lands, inhabited by Indians who had known no contact with the white man, people who spoke another language altogether. The Cree came to call their northern Athapaskan neighbours, no doubt somewhat derisively, *Otchipiweons*, meaning "pointed skins," probably referring to the way in which the northern Indians — when they were first drawn into the fur trade — dried their beaver skins. Their pelts were considered inferior by both the more adept trappers among the Crees and the white traders for whom the beaver were trapped. Taken from the Cree name, the English derivative "Chipewyan" dates only to the late eighteenth century, after contact with white fur traders. In any case, it was not their own name. To the people themselves, in their own language, they were *Dene*, "the people." Among them, the Chipewyan around the upper Thelon whose livelihood was based on the barrenland caribou, were known specifically as *ethen-eldili-dene*, "caribou- eating people."

In 1715, William Stuart was sent from the Hudson's Bay Company post at York Factory overland to the west. He entered territory never before seen by a white man, guided by a Chipewyan woman named Thanadelthur. Her story survived, partly through H.B.C. journals, but largely through the oral tradition of her people.

In the spring of 1713, a band of Crees raided a Chipewyan camp. The Cree had guns, so their success was inevitable, and they marched home to their camp on the Nelson River with their war prize: at least three strong, beautiful, young Chipewyan women, among them Thanadelthur. The women were kept as slaves and one can only imagine what their duties might have included, given the treatment normally afforded to women by Cree men, even among their own bands. It is not surprising that women captives frequently tried to escape, occasionally dying in the process.

Thanadelthur and another young Chipewyan woman fled their Cree masters in the fall of 1714 and set out to cross the unknown country back to their own people. They had only the most meagre of supplies, whatever small game they could catch in a snare. The weather turned cold. Desperately hungry, they eventually turned back from their northward march, hoping against hope that they might find the white men, the traders. The Cree had boasted to the young women about these traders, and Thanadelthur herself had seen all the amazing new things which the Cree were using. They searched in vain, until Thanadelthur's companion finally could go no farther. She died a frozen death. Thanadelthur struggled on for just a few more days and, as luck would have it, stumbled across some tracks in the snow which led into a camp of white men. On November 24, she was taken to the post at York Factory.

James Knight, the Governor at York Factory beside the mouth of the Nelson River, was immediately impressed with this determined and intelligent young woman. In Thanadelthur he saw a useful ally, as he already had in mind making contact with the Chipewyans to further the trade. The problem was that the Chipewyans were justifiably afraid of the Crees and, therefore, unlikely to be tempted to travel through Cree country to reach York Factory. Knight's solution had two parts: he would establish a new trading post farther to the northwest, at the mouth of the Churchill River, and he would mediate a peace between the rival Indians.

In June of 1715 — by which time Thanadelthur had been at the post for more than six months — everything was set. The Cree had agreed to send a peace delegation into the territory of the northern Indians. Knight selected his Cree-speaking protege, William Stuart, to accompany the mission. Stuart was charged with the responsibility of ensuring Thanadelthur's safety. "The Slave Woman," as she was known, carried several presents from Knight to be distributed among her people, as an enticement to the trade.

The delegation that left York Factory on June 27 was about 150 strong. It took until early August just to reach the Churchill River, by which time most of the Indians were ill. Some turned back to York Factory. Many of the Cree suffered on the long trek across the barrenlands, and several died. The party broke up into small bands, as more Indians gave up the mission. Some killed their dogs for food, others survived on moss.

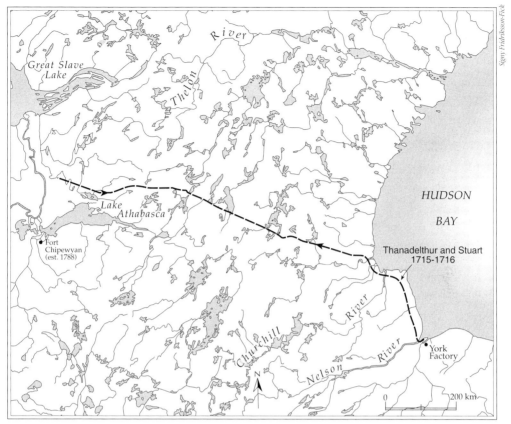

Thanadelthur's Country

In October, Stuart sent a note with some Indians who were turning back. He was only a hundred miles beyond the Churchill River and, he reported, "Wee are in a Starving Condition at this time   Wee still push on in our Journey   Wee have eat nothing this 8 days   I do not think as I shall see you any more but I have a good heart."

Thanadelthur, Stuart, and a dozen Crees did push on. Eventually they crossed the barrenlands to reach the wooded country to the west, near the headwaters of the Thelon River. Later in the winter, having found no one as yet, they came across a camp with the bodies of nine dead Chipewyans, Thanadelthur's people, clearly murdered by a party of Cree raiders. It was, reported Stuart, a horrifying scene of massacre. The mission seemed doomed. Stuart could not persuade the Crees to go on; they feared retaliation by any Chipewyans they might encounter.

So Thanadelthur carried on alone, having implored the Cree delegation to wait and give her ten days to find her people. They waited nervously. She followed the tracks of her countrymen and found a band of 400 Chipewyans gathering for revenge. She talked persuasively. On the tenth day, Thanadelthur and two emissaries appeared at the Cree camp. 160 other Chipewyans remained hidden until the signal was given. With Thanadelthur's urging, a peace was forged. The rival Indians sat together and smoked the pipe of peace.

A delegation of ten Chipewyans joined Stuart's party and, together with the Crees, they returned to York Factory on May 7, 1716, just short of a year from their departure. They had travelled a distance in excess of 2,500 kilometres as the crow flies, actually much farther given the vagaries of the country. Thanadelthur was received as a hero, rightfully given most of the credit for securing the peace and introducing her people to the fur trade at Hudson Bay. Knight's plan had been realized. More exciting even than that, for Knight, he noticed that the Chipewyans who returned to York Factory had knives and ornaments of copper.

Thanadelthur died the following winter at York Factory, still a young woman, still much esteemed by Governor James Knight. By then she had filled Knight's mind with thoughts of copper and gold to be found, she said, in the farthest reaches of her people's territory. That dream was not to be forgotten.

———————◆————————

As the 18th century progressed, word spread among the Ethen-eldili, the Caribou-Eaters, of the peace with the Crees to the south, and of the white man's trading post to the east. For these people of the forest-tundra zone around the headwaters of the Thelon, this was the beginning of contact with the world beyond their own horizon. But even as their Chipewyan cousins to the southeast were drawn into increasing contact, the Ethen-eldili remained detached, continuing their established way of life, dependent largely on the caribou for all their needs. A trading journey to the Hudson's Bay post at the mouth of the Churchill River would take two or three years, and white man's gadgets were just not that vital.

Yet the Hudson's Bay Company's dream of finding a source of copper and gold to the northwest persisted. Another young British trader was despatched in pursuit of the dream. In 1772 Samuel Hearne became the second white man, after William Stuart, to make the long trek overland from the distant trading posts on Hudson Bay through Chipewyan territory. On his way to the mouth of the Coppermine River on the arctic coast, accompanied by a large band of Chipewyans with their renowned leader Matonabbee, Hearne passed through the land of the Ethen-eldili. His route took him across the uppermost reaches of the Thelon drainage, though precisely where is uncertain. But his journal contains telling passages detailing the earliest information received from Indians about the Thelon.

"As the current sets to the northeastward, it empties itself, in all probability, into some part of Hudson bay, and, from the latitude, no part seems more likely for this communication than Baker's lake, at the head of Chesterfield inlet. This, however, is mere conjecture, nor is it of any consequence as navigation on any of the rivers in those parts is not only impracticable, but would be also unprofitable, as they do not lead into a country that produces anything for trade, or that contains any inhabitants worth visiting.

"Matonabbee assured me that for more than a generation past one family [possibly one band] only have taken up their winter abode in those woods, which are situated so far on the barren-ground as to be quite out of track of any other Indians," Hearne continued in his journal. "The situation is said to be remarkably favourable for every kind of game that the barren-ground produces at the different seasons of the year. Few of the trading Northern Indians have visited this place; but those who have, give a pleasing description of it, all agreeing that it is situated on the banks of a river which has communication with several fine lakes.

"The few who compose this little commonwealth, are by long custom, and the constant example of their forefathers, possessed of a provident turn of mind, with a degree of frugality unknown to every other tribe of Indians in this country except the Esquimaux. Deer is said to visit this part of the country in astonishing numbers, both in spring and autumn, of which circumstance the inhabitants avail themselves by killing and drying as much of their flesh as possible, particularly in the fall of the year, so they are seldom in want of a good winter's stock. Geese, ducks and swans visit here in great plenty during their migration, both in the spring and fall, and by much art, joined to an insurmountable patience, are caught in considerable numbers in snares, and without doubt make a very pleasing change of food. It is also reported, though I confess I doubt the truth of it, that a remarkable species of partridge, as large as English fowls, are found in that part of the country only.

"The rivers and lakes near the little forest where the family above mentioned had fixed their abode abounded with fine fish," he reported, "particularly trout and barbel which are easily caught, the former with hooks, and the latter in nets. In fact, I have not seen or heard of any part of this country which seems to possess half the advantages requisite for a constant residence, that are ascribed to this little spot."

For a man who never saw the place, Hearne was remarkably accurate in his assessment of what was, from white man's perspective, a vast uncharted territory and a total mystery, the *The-lew-dezeth*, meaning "Fish River," the Chipewyan name for the Thelon.

In 1781, a smallpox epidemic ravaged the Cree population, killing thousands, and spread to large numbers of those Chipewyans who lived in closer proximity to the Cree. The more remote Caribou-Eaters escaped with far fewer lives lost. That was only the beginning, however, for later waves of scarlet fever, influenza, measles and tuberculosis took their toll even among the Ethen-eldili. By then, contact with white man was well established, after the fur trade moved inland from Hudson Bay.

In 1788, the North West Company built the first trading post in the northern interior, appropriately named Fort Chipewyan, at the southwest end of Lake Athabasca. This post was moved to the north shore in 1800 and in 1821, when the rival trading companies merged, that post was taken over by the Hudson's Bay Company.

Some years after Hearne, another explorer named George Back passed just to the west of the upper Thelon country, on his way to the arctic coast down what we now know as the Back River. In 1834, he met a party of Indians near Great Slave Lake, one of whom drew a map of the route to *The-lew-dezeth* and described its wooded banks.

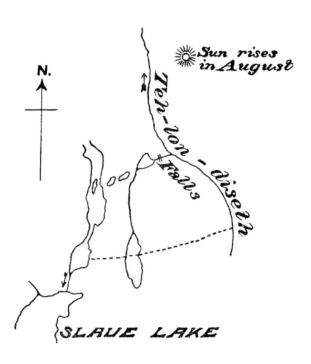

Map drawn by a Chipewyan hunter for George Back, at Fort Resolution, 1833

White man, by this time, knew of the Thelon country but had still never set eyes upon it. The mystery persisted, as it did for many years yet. Not until the end of the century did a white man finally travel into the Thelon valley. For European explorers, the secrets of the Thelon remained unknown until about one hundred years ago today.

3

The Explorers

It is one of the remarkable facts of the Thelon's history that the first white man to travel on the river above Beverly Lake, did so by canoe going *upstream*. It stems, perhaps, from the general sweep of northern exploration,* from east to west.

The mouth of the Thelon, at Chesterfield Inlet, was first charted in 1747 by a privately funded expedition under Captain William Moor, sailing up the west coast of Hudson Bay. Later, in 1761, the Hudson's Bay Company sent another man, William Christopher, to explore Chesterfield Inlet; he sailed up into Baker Lake hoping in vain to find the long sought Northwest Passage. When it did not serve that purpose, it was all but forgotten, certainly long ignored.

In 1899, 35-year-old David Hanbury arrived at Fort Churchill on his way to explore the Thelon. He was a well-educated British adventurer, with training in surveying and geology, but he insisted that his aim was "sport and travel, no attempt having been made to accomplish elaborate geographical or other scientific work." He was, it became clear, a man of indomitable spirit.

Before the *real* journey began, Hanbury travelled overland, mostly by dog-sled, through a Manitoba winter to reach Fort Churchill on the Hudson Bay coast in early April. At the time, it was the last outpost of civilization, however basic. Wisely, some weeks were spent on final preparations. On May 12, 1899, a party of four on two sleighs with twelve dogs headed north across the ice of Hudson Bay. Hanbury was accompanied by "two trustworthy Red River half-breeds" whom he had hired in Winnipeg, and a local Eskimo named Miluk who knew the country well.

* *"Exploration" and "discovery" are used throughout the book with reference to the white man. The author acknowledges the long-standing use and occupation of these lands by Native people.*

Hanbury's party on the way north from Fort Churchill, May 1899

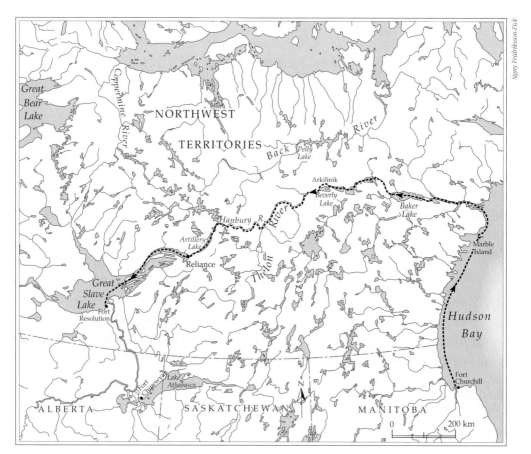

Route followed by D. Hanbury, 1899

They reached Marble Island, more than 500 kilometres to the north, on June 5. "Except for one blizzard, we had had glorious weather, the air clear and cold, and the surface of the ice as dry as in mid-winter, but we were in straits for supplies," Hanbury wrote. "Fortunately, we found and killed a few deer [caribou], the mainstay of the traveller on the 'Barren Ground,' just in time to save us from an ignominious retreat." At Marble Island they picked up a canoe cached there the previous summer, and continued on immediately across the ice to Chesterfield Inlet. There, at last, caribou were plentiful, but the ice conditions worsened, "so rough that the dogs' feet were cut almost to pieces." Nevertheless, on June 21, they arrived at the head of the Inlet, where the current exits from Baker Lake.

Further travel was prevented by break-up; there was neither solid ice for sled travel, nor open water for boats. So Hanbury and his men stayed with local Inuit, who welcomed the visitors. In early July, there was open water enough to proceed with difficulty. Travel was slow. It was July 19 when the party reached the west end of Baker Lake, and the mouth of the Thelon River, which Hanbury called the Ark-i-linik after the Inuit reference to some hills north of Beverly Lake.[*] They tracked upstream and pushed on across the big lakes, despite being impeded by ice right to the end of July. The route, so far, was the reverse of that already travelled by the first white men, the Tyrrell brothers. In 1893, J.B. and J.W. Tyrrell had descended and mapped the Dubawnt River from northern Saskatchewan, to join the Thelon at the east end of Beverly Lake, from where they continued downstream out to Hudson Bay.

"We had now entered the unexplored country," wrote Hanbury, looking ahead to the ascent of the Thelon, above the Dubawnt. "How far west the Ark-i-linik River would take us, and whether it was navigable for canoes, were problems which we had come to solve. There was no information to be obtained from the Eskimo, for none of them had ever ascended the river for any distance. So, without guides and without supplies of any kind, we started into this unknown country, trusting to our rifles and nets to provide us with a living, and to the good fortune which, up till now, had attended us."

Accompanied now by two Baker Lake Inuit in their kayaks, Hanbury and his "two trustworthy Red River half-breeds" paddled their canoe up the Thelon. Hanbury delighted at seeing musk-oxen, and commented on the amount of spruce to be found beside the river. Somewhere along the way, the Inuit turned back toward home, and Hanbury's single canoe forged ahead into unknown territory, "a stretch of country about eighty miles in length into which no human being enters. The Eskimo do not hunt so far west, and Yellow Knives and Dog Ribs [Indians] from Slave Lake do not go so far east." Somewhat prophetically, he

The Inuit of the Thelon valley, around Beverly and Aberdeen Lakes, were known as Akilingmiut in their own tongue.

added, "To penetrate this country in the dead of winter would be simply to court starvation. Then the deer have all departed, and to depend on finding musk-oxen at the end of the journey would be risky indeed."

In what is probably the first identification of the Thelon as something of a sanctuary for the musk-oxen, Hanbury continued in his prophetic way. "There still remains, I am happy to say, one spot in this Great Barren North land — which is sacred to the musk-ox — into which human beings dare not enter. Here the animals remain in their primeval state, their solitude undisturbed by the hated sound and sight of man. Long may they remain so." Hanbury would be proved correct on more than one count.

When he reached a fork in his route, the explorer chose the branch which we now know as the Hanbury River, and eventually made it over the height of land and back into charted territory at Clinton-Colden Lake. In his estimation, it was not a difficult trip, albeit upstream. In fact, he wrote, "the journey eventually turned out to be so absurdly easy, that I more than once regretted that it was so, for half the pleasure of exploration is derived from meeting and surmounting difficulties." This despite an accident on the Lockhart River near the end of his journey which almost left the party destitute.

"In letting the canoe down a small side rapid by a bow-and-stern line, the stern line parted, and the tail of the canoe was quickly swung out into the current. In an instant it was caught by the rapids, and the bow line wrenched from the grasp of the man who held it. It all happened in a second.... The waters ahead, toward which the small canoe was being hurried, were all white, one broad expanse of seething foam, from which the tops of black rocks protruded in ominous fashion." A day later, following on downstream with no more than the clothes on their backs, they spotted the canoe on the far bank, built a raft and recovered the essential vessel plus one box of their outfit. Fortunately, it contained Hanbury's note-books and diaries. But his geological and botanical specimens, their rifles and fish-nets, and all his unprecedented photographs were lost.

Nevertheless, by late September he was at Fort Resolution on Great Slave Lake, and in due course he returned south and home to England. But his appetite was only whetted by the "absurdly easy" experience; Hanbury was soon to return, next time in search of greater adventure.

Just three months after David Hanbury passed through Edmonton on his way out of the country, James Tyrrell arrived there from the east, and set about preparing his party for their venture into the Thelon.

Tyrrell was a surveyor. He had accompanied his brother J.B., the geologist, on descents of both the Dubawnt and the Kazan just a few years earlier. But the principal

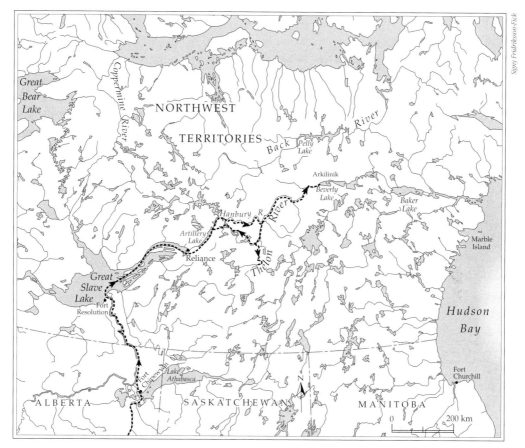

Signy Fridriksson-Fick

Route followed by J.W. Tyrrell, 1900

purpose this time was strictly to explore and map, so the Surveyor General in Ottawa called upon J.W. At the time he received the request, "in the hands of an Indian courier," the younger Tyrrell was working on a survey of timber lands in northern Ontario. He lost no time in complying.

The party consisted of nine men. In Winnipeg, on the way west, Tyrrell engaged Robert Bear and John Kipling, "two half-breed voyageurs from the St. Peter's reserve." In Edmonton he added Percy Acres as cook, Pierre French and Harry Monette, two expert canoemen he knew from the earlier barrenland expeditions. Later, in Fort Chipewyan, another voyageur was hired, a Chipewyan named Toura. A surveyor from Ontario, C.C. Fairchild, came along to assist with the fieldwork, and Archdeacon Lofthouse, whom Tyrrell had met in Churchill, completed the team.

Their wilderness quest began literally at the end of the road 290 kilometres north of Edmonton. On February 26, 1900, five heavily laden dog-sleds pulled away from the

Tyrrell's expedition dog-teams leaving Edmonton

The Tyrrell expedition en route north from Edmonton

The expedition at Fort Chipewyan

James W. Tyrrell at Fort Reliance, 1900

Hudson's Bay Company post, to begin a journey by sled and canoe of 7,360 kilometres. By early May, after a difficult but ordinary — for the time — trip north, the nine men and about three tons of equipment reached Pike's Portage* at the eastern extremity of Great Slave Lake. The dogs' work was finished; those that had survived were sent back to Fort Resolution. Henceforth, the party advanced strictly under its own power, at first pulling the sleds over candled ice, and then by canoe.

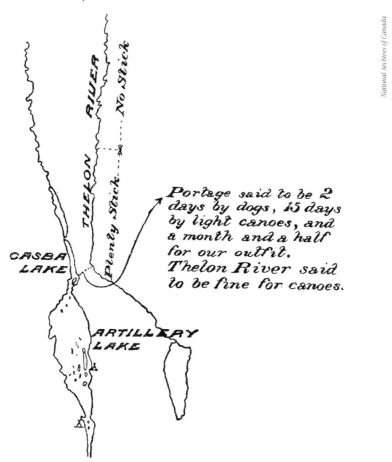

Map drawn by Pierre Ft. Smith, May 31ˢᵗ, 1900, with notations added by JW Tyrrell

By June 18 there was enough open water to allow their advance up Artillery Lake, and they retraced David Hanbury's route in reverse, though there is no evidence to suggest that they had any mapped information from him. Tyrrell apparently relied on the 66-year-old

* Named after Warburton Pike, who used it in 1890, this became the standard route between Great Slave Lake and the more elevated Artillery Lake, for travellers to and from the barrenlands.

sketch map that an Indian had drawn for George Back. And, fortunately, he too met an Indian, Pierre Fort Smith, familiar enough with the country to draw his own version, not substantially different from the earlier one.

Once over the height of land and into the Thelon system, Tyrrell's party moved as quickly as the mapping duties permitted. At a hill beside Sifton Lake, in the upper reaches of the Hanbury River, on June 27th, he and Fairchild spotted some musk-oxen. Despite the late hour, they went in pursuit of fresh meat. For Tyrrell, it proved to be a most remarkable spectacle, which he mentioned frequently in years to come. His cook, Percy Acres, and a young musk-ox bull ended up playing a version of ring-around-the-rosie about a huge boulder. Even at 1:30 in the morning, there was enough light for Tyrrell to get a photograph of the incident. Today, the maps mark the place as Muskox Hill.

This branch of the river he named after Hanbury, perhaps begrudgingly acknowledging "the first white man to ascend it," in what proves to be Tyrrell's only reference to his predecessor on the river. The three canoes reached the junction with the main branch of the Thelon on the morning of July 7. Subsequently he comments on the validity of Hearne's second-hand description of the river valley, offering his own observations as confirmation of former Indian habitation. Indeed, farther downstream, he documented the remnants of former Indian camps, including at least one standing tipi frame. He also remarked that nearly all the musk-oxen sighted were found on the north bank of the river, a suggestion consistent with most modern-day experience.

Just where the river exits sharply out of the widening around what is now known as Ursus Islands, and heads straight east toward Beverly Lake, Tyrrell encountered people for the first time. "The encampment consisted of three or four lodges, and thirty-three souls in all, chief amongst whom was an old coast Eskimo, named Ping-a-wa-look, commonly known by the traders at Fort Churchill as 'Cheesecloth.' With him, as well as with one or two others our archdeacon was acquainted, and one of them had met me in 1893, so we found ourselves amongst warm friends."

On Beverly Lake, waiting out a ferocious barrenlands storm, Tyrrell made a decision to split the party, knowing that he had very nearly reached the point where the Dubawnt River — which he had paddled in 1893 — joins the Thelon. Fairchild, Lofthouse and four of the voyageurs were to continue the mapping on down to Chesterfield Inlet, concentrating on those sides of the larger lakes which Tyrrell had not surveyed in 1893. Then, as his instructions read, they were to return upstream by the same route, making sure to arrive back at Fort Reliance by September 15. Tyrrell, together with the remaining voyageurs Robert Bear and Toura, headed back upstream determined to explore the uncharted main branch of

While Tyrrell paddled some of the time, at other times, he sat in the middle of the canoe engaged in his mapping

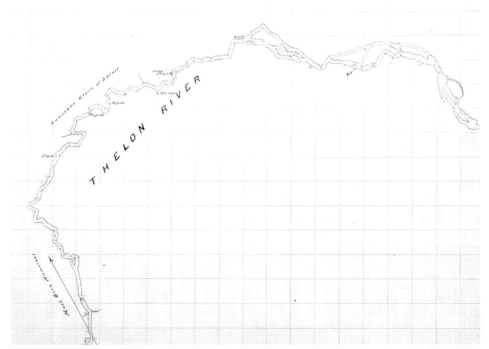

Tyrrell's map of "the big bend" stretch of the Thelon River, roughly mid-way between the Hanbury junction and Beverly Lake

Tyrrell first encountered Inuit along the Thelon at Pingawalook's camp, near Ursus Islands.

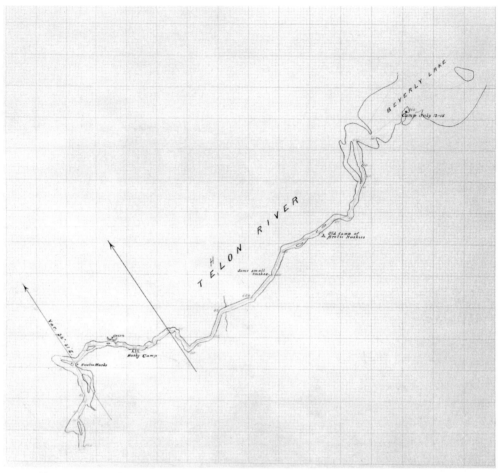

Tyrrell's map of the stretch of the Thelon River from Ursus Islands down to Beverly Lake

JW Tyrrell/Thomas Fisher Library

the Thelon, upstream of the Hanbury-Thelon junction. The two groups parted company on July 16.

At Pingawalook's camp, Tyrrell traded for some moccasins. "They were much needed before we got out of the country, for as my men tracked the canoe up stream, the sharp rocks and stones over which they had to walk, cut through two or three pairs of shoes a day." Nevertheless, on the 28th they reached the Hanbury-Thelon junction, and three days later headed upriver into unknown country, on the main branch of the Thelon.

On August 9, the upstream march, "obstructed in several places by shallow rapids," reached the confluence with the Elk River. Neither fork appealed to Tyrrell, with "both branches rapid and shallow." And so, "judging from my progress during the last two weeks,

Tyrrell ascended the upper Thelon, above the Hanbury junction, with voyageurs Robert Bear and Toura

and the prospect of increased difficulties ahead, I came to the conclusion that it would be unwise to attempt to push through to Lake Athabasca." Instead, he returned back downstream about half-way to the Hanbury junction, where he remembered seeing a small stream joining from the west. That, he thought, might provide a route over the divide, back toward Great Slave, via Artillery where they had begun paddling two months before. The stream, however, was too small; only a few miles up it, there was not enough water to float the canoe. Tyrrell, as ever, was decisive.

"I decided to send my two men with the canoe, around by the way we had come, to Artillery lake, and that I would walk across alone.

"It seemed that there could be no great difficulty in doing so, for the distance in a straight line I knew [from his own surveying] to be only about eighty miles; the season was

still early and there were now plenty of deer roving over the country. Thus viewing the problem, I sent my men back with the canoe and its contents, and having selected my necessary outfit for the tramp, bundled it up into a neat pack of about fifty pounds and started off. It did not feel heavy at first, and the weather being fine I made fair progress, but as the day wore on, my pack became burdensome and by evening I was quite ready to lay it down and creep into my sleeping bag. This first day's march, which covered thirteen miles, was along the course of the stream, [and] took me to the shore of a small lake, which of itself formed no serious obstruction to travel. Because of the irregularities of the shore and the

Tyrrell setting out alone on his long trek overland from the upper Thelon to Artillery Lake

impossibility of seeing any great distance ahead, it required a twelve mile tramp to get free from this lake, and that represented my second day's journey. My rations were obtained from the carcass of a deer which I had shot, and some biscuits which I had brought in my pack.

"On the morning of my third day, only three miles from my 'camp' I came upon a large lake — to which I have taken the liberty of attaching my own name — since I am sure it has never been, and perhaps never will be, of as much interest to any one else as it proved to me."

It was far from an easy trek. He was impeded by large lakes — the largest named after himself — and streams too cold and swift to swim across. He tramped through muskeg up to the ankles. His moccasins, from Pingawalook's camp, were soon worn out; he resorted to removing the sleeves from his jacket and wrapping them around his feet. After five days he had moved west only 25 kilometres. There remained, by his own calculation, more than 100 kilometres ahead to the shore of Artillery Lake. Then the weather turned sour, and his real trouble began.

"The morning of my sixth day set in with a chilling northeast wind and pelting rain, which not only saturated my clothing, but also the moss, so that I could make no fire. Having a small flask of brandy with me, I refreshed myself with a little of it, in water, and a biscuit, and tramped on, making thirteen miles during the day. The night being dark at this season, it was not possible to travel continuously, so, wet and shivering as I was, I lay down on the rocks in the pelting rain to try and sleep, but this was not to be, for my bed soon became a puddle of water, and I was uncomfortable indeed. I earnestly longed for the daylight, so that I might get up and travel, and at length it came, but still the cold rain came down, so that I could only wring out my single blanket and start on without breakfast. A deer skin which I carried in addition to my blanket had become so water-soaked as to be too heavy to carry and was left behind."

The next day, the sun came out at mid-day and Tyrrell managed to shoot a caribou, so his circumstances improved dramatically. However, he still had a long walk ahead. And by late August in the barrenlands, the weather can become very unstable. Tyrrell knew this well enough; he and his brother only just escaped with their lives from their first barrenland expedition seven years earlier in 1893, when they were caught by the onset of early winter weather. Now, on his lonely trek west across unmapped country, he kept a watchful eye on the sky.

"Observing the approach of a heavy storm, I proceeded to fortify myself as well as my blanket and canvas wrapper would admit of, and so fairly well weathered out a bad night. But the next day was intolerable. I endeavoured to push on, but so cold and drenching was the rain that I shivered even as I travelled, under my watersoaked burden. Later in the day the weather became so thick, that I was as one walking in the dark — not knowing what was before me — and soon found myself almost entirely surrounded by water. I was now forced to await an improvement in the weather, and so, partaking of a wet biscuit, for I had nothing dry, and a drink of brandy, I lay down on the sand.

"All night the cold rain came down in torrents, so that I was perfectly saturated with it. As the morning dawned conditions were not improved, for the rain had changed to snow and clothed the landscape in her chilling garment of white. It left me in an extremely uncomfortable condition, to say the least, being without shelter, fire or cooked food, but the worst seemed to have passed, for at eleven o'clock the next day the sunlight broke forth again and brought me much needed relief."

It was now August 22, and Tyrrell found himself retracing his steps back up a long peninsula and working his way slowly around a large lake. Through all this, despite the conditions and his own miserable state, he somehow managed to keep a careful and detailed account of the land, and produce sketches from which he could ultimately draw the first official maps of this territory with remarkable accuracy. The next day brought another storm.

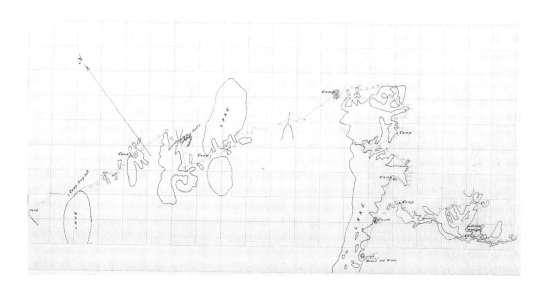

Tyrrell's map of the overland route from the upper Thelon River to Artillery Lake

JW Tyrrell/Thomas Fisher Library

"A gale from the northeast, with driving rain and sleet — so severe that I was forced to seek shelter, which to some extent I found on the lee side of a rock. Here I spread my canvas and, wrapping my wet blanket about me, remained for two days until the storm of wind, rain and snow had spent its fury. My biscuits were now all gone, and the only available stimulant I had at this camp was the remainder of my flask of brandy, of which I gladly availed myself.

"My condition had become decidedly serious. I had not slept a night since I had left my canoe, and this wretched weather and lack of food was already telling seriously upon me. The barren ground is a most inhospitable place in bad weather, but having exposed myself to its inhospitality there was only one thing for me to do, and that was to get out again as best I could, and this I was quite resolved to do."

At the end of August, nearly spent himself, Tyrrell reached the shore of Artillery Lake, and found a cache he had left there in June. Of the comforts that implies, he says only that he made "a snug camp in the spruce grove," and leaves to the imagination the pleasures of once again being warm, dry and nourished.

Two days later, Robert Bear and Toura, his two voyageurs, paddled into camp having completed their ascent of the Hanbury River. Only a few days after that, Fairchild and his party arrived in Artillery Lake, having been all the way out to Hudson Bay and back. Reunited, the expedition headed south. It took three months to reach Edmonton, by canoe, steamer, and dog-sled.

Tyrrell's mapping of the territory east of Great Slave Lake — in all he set down 2,766 kilometres of new survey — became the basis for the official maps of Canada for many years to follow, until his job was taken over by aerial surveying. It is as an explorer and a map-maker, therefore, that he is remembered. But equally noteworthy is a single paragraph in his final report to Ottawa, in which he joined David Hanbury in advising that "for the preservation of the musk-oxen — which may be so easily slaughtered — and are already rapidly diminishing in numbers, I would suggest that the territory between the Thelon and Back rivers be set apart by the Government as a game preserve."

Of the many names[*] put onto the map by James W. Tyrrell, perhaps the most celebrated was the Hanbury River, after the first white man to travel it. Sometime over the winter following his return, Tyrrell communicated his act of commemoration to the Englishman, who called it "an honour for which I thank him, but for which I was not at all anxious." Nevertheless, the name has endured. In a peculiar twist of history, David Hanbury returned to his river once again the next year, 1901.

He wanted to spend a year among the Inuit, for more "sport and travel." Having approached through Churchill previously, he decided to go north from Edmonton to Great

* See Appendix II: Gazeteer of the Thelon Valley

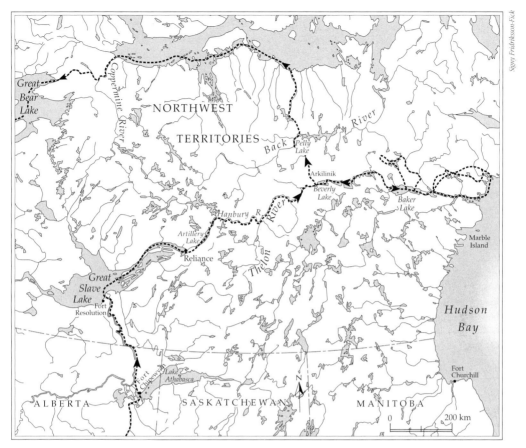

Signy Fridriksson-Fick

Route followed by D. Hanbury, 1901-02

Slave Lake, and then east to the Thelon and downstream to Hudson Bay, reversing his route from 1899. By late July, 1901, Hanbury's party was carrying their outfit, including two large Peterborough canoes, over Pike's Portage. Joining him on this venture was Sandy Turner, a Métis from Edmonton, and a young Englishman named Hubert Darrell, who had been swept up in the goldrush to the Klondike and stayed in the north. With the assistance of some Indians hired as voyageurs, they were launched onto the upper reaches of the Hanbury River on July 27. In due course, the Indians returned to Great Slave; thus it is probably fair to say that Hanbury was the first white man to actually paddle himself down the Thelon.

Hanbury and his two companions spent that autumn and winter among his "Husky friends" around Baker Lake and Chesterfield Inlet, preparing for a winter sled trip across the barrenlands northwest to the arctic coast. It must have been quite a sight when the expedition pulled away from their igloos at the east end of Baker Lake in early March. In addition to the three visitors, there were several Inuit men, with their multiple wives and numerous children all walking alongside the three heavily loaded sleighs. One sled bore Hanbury's two canoes, the 19-footer nested inside the slightly larger one. Twenty dogs, in all, did the work.

Hanbury spent the winter of 1901-02 with a group of Baker Lake Inuit, including Ameryah and Uttungerlah

Their route took them back up the Thelon valley as far as Tivialik (Beverly Lake), where they headed straight north toward the Back River, across Pelly Lake to the arctic coast. They travelled by sled along the coast until the beginning of July. Eventually, by canoe, they reached the Coppermine River, which they ascended. Hanbury, Darrell and Turner went on over the divide to Great Bear Lake and the Mackenzie basin. The three Inuit men turned around to go home, collecting their families along the way where they had stayed in other camps. Hanbury reached Fort Norman, on the Mackenzie River, at the end of August, 1902.

This journey, like his previous one, was an epic, of the sort previously undertaken by such notable arctic travellers as Samuel Hearne and John Rae. Hanbury was the first recreational traveller in the barrenlands, and he will never be equalled.

Between them, Hanbury and Tyrrell brought a huge territory to the attention of white man. What had been an unknown land of dark secrets was now mapped, photographed and described in the literature. As the twentieth century began, the land of the Thelon valley became part of the reality of universal knowledge, that which binds us to it even today. Hanbury and Tyrrell, together, opened the door into the valley of the Thelon.

Among the first to take advantage of this new knowledge was the Royal North West Mounted Police. The Mounties had already established a presence in remote parts of the Arctic, including a post at Fullerton just north of Chesterfield Inlet on Hudson Bay. In 1908, the time had come to confirm their jurisdiction over the vast inland territory to the west, an area bisected by the Thelon River.

Inspector Ephrem Albert Pelletier led the expedition, accompanied by three other Mounties. In fact, they were the first white men to travel the entire route without employing Native guides or canoemen. The four Mounties, in two 18-foot Peterborough canoes, paddled and sailed from Fort Resolution on Great Slave Lake, via the standard route — over Pike's Portage, up Artillery Lake and north to Clinton-Colden, then over the height of land to the headwaters of the Hanbury, and down it to the Thelon — a distance of two thousand kilometres, to the mouth of Chesterfield Inlet.

It was, to date, the longest and most difficult patrol in Mounted Police history. That it was later overshadowed by others, most often because of their tragic outcomes, is really only a measure of the efficiency and competence with which Pelletier conducted his assignment. The actual trip was uneventful, although it is noteworthy that they saw only three musk-oxen along the entire river. Not until the entrance to Beverly Lake did they meet any other people on the river. Pelletier's journal documents this encounter with the most inland of all the Inuit.

"On approaching the shore I called out 'Chimo! Chimo!' which is the usual form of greeting when meeting Eskimos in these lands. We were much surprised to hear a 'Good Morning' in answer. [Constable] Walker expressed his astonishment by saying 'Holy Smoke!' to which the native, misconstruing his meaning, replied very fervently: 'Me no smoke; me no tabacco!' We made a landing, and I discovered that the Chief of the camp was Ameryah, commonly known as Lucky Moore. He speaks good English; he is one of the natives who accompanied Hanbury on his long voyage to the Arctic coast and up the Coppermine River in 1901-02. The canoe Hanbury gave him he still had, very carefully hauled on the beach. He was well dressed with white men's clothes, and had very little the appearance of a native ...

"He was much interested in the maps I had, and recognized with great glee and gusto every prominent point on the tracing, which speaks highly for the maps made by J.W. Tyrrell. We gave them a few presents of tobacco, matches, needles, hooks, knives, etc. in return for which they gave us a few deerskin coats and boots ... They all expressed wonder at seeing no Indians or natives accompanying us."

The stated purpose of Pelletier's expedition was "to report on the location and condition of Indian and Eskimo bands, and to appraise the need to establish permanent [Mounted Police] posts along the route." His own report from 1908 sums up the successful findings.

"The route between Great Slave Lake and the Hudson's Bay, although not presenting any serious difficulties is by no means an easy one. The Hanbury River is the most dangerous stretch.

"As to using this route as a permanent yearly patrol, the time is not yet ripe for it. There is no one living on the longer part of this stretch. The natives themselves, first the Yellow Knives and Dog Rib Indians, yearly come to Fort Resolution. They seem to be well off and hold a fairly good reputation. They have no permanent camp, and a police detachment would do them no good.

"Secondly, the Eskimos at the Hudson's Bay end of the route are very few and far between. They are well provided with arms, ammunition and trading goods, which they procure either from the Hudson's Bay Company or the whalers in the Hudson's Bay. There is no crime committed by these people, although totally ignorant of the law and Christianity, they have old customs and laws of their own which are very fair and Christianlike in every respect ..."

As a result, no immediate action was taken. However, it was not very many years before two police posts were established to serve the region: at Baker Lake to the east and Fort Reliance to the west. In due course, the Mounted Police were to return to the Thelon valley, but not until mysterious reports of death and murder compelled them to do so.

4

The Trappers

The trapper was a tough, wiry man, not gaunt, but certainly not over-fed. With an easy gait he loped along beside the sled, piled high with furs, pulled by a team of six dogs. The dogs, too, looked as though they could use a good meal, but their energy nonetheless was impressive. Dogs and master appeared worn, weathered, and bedraggled, yet ready to take on anything that confronted them. They had come a long way; that was obvious, even as the little ensemble moved across the ice of Great Slave Lake and up onto the shore, where the spring snow was getting soft in the warm afternoon sun. It was nearing the end of April.

The trapper yelled "Whoaa!" and the dogs pulled up short, right in front of the Hudson's Bay Company trading post in Fort Resolution, the northernmost outpost of civilization. A small cluster of men gathered about the trader, local Indians and other trappers who had been working traplines to the south of Great Slave for some years now. The new arrival, his grizzled face unshaved and wind-burned, looked round the circle and recognized the others, all of whom he had seen seven or eight months earlier at this same post. Since then, he had seen not another single human being. He said nothing.

Then, one of the other trappers asked "Where d'ya get to?" and everyone waited in silence, for they had heard of his plans.

"I spent the winter up on the barrenlands, in the country by the Thelon," said the old hand, "where there were more white foxes than you've ever seen." And that, perhaps, is how it all began, or close to it.

That is conjecture, in part. The first white trapper, in fact, to work the area around Artillery Lake was Jack Stark in 1914. Several trappers ventured up onto the barrenlands east of Great Slave in search of white foxes shortly after the First World War. They called it "the Country." In 1924 the white foxes came in droves; one legend claims a single trapper northeast of Great Slave Lake caught 900 that year. In 1925 the Hudson's Bay Company established a new post at Snowdrift, farther east on Great Slave Lake than Fort Resolution. By 1926, according to one veteran trapper on his way to the barrenlands, "there are only ten or twelve white trappers who have penetrated its depths." Every spring thereafter they brought their accumulated furs out to Snowdrift to trade.

The cycle began in the autumn, before freeze-up. The trapper, alone or with a single partner, assembled his outfit. Every item was essential, nothing surplus, for everything had to be carried. The lot — traps, staple foods, pots and pans, tents, rifles, ammunition, fish nets, dog harness, sled and dogs — was loaded into a canoe. The trapper pushed his canoe off from the shore in front of the trading post, and headed east, threading through the islands of Great Slave Lake, bound for the Thelon wilderness, or as the trappers said, "the Country."

To survive, the trapper needed to find two things: caribou and wood. The strategy was straightforward enough, but far from simple: find a wooded patch sufficient to build a log cabin, cut enough firewood to last the winter, and be ready when the caribou migration came through sometime in October. With only an axe, a bag of spikes, and a lot of muscle, the trapper would fell and strip the trees, move them into place one atop the other, stuff moss into the cracks, and in no more than two weeks have his cabin ready.

Next came the quest for food. There was not only himself to feed, but the dogs — dogs upon whom he would need to depend for his life during the coming winter. If the caribou were not yet in the area, then fish nets were set and tended daily. The fish could be hung and dried, ready as dog-food for the long winter months. Fishing was much easier now, with open water, or even with early winter's thin ice, than it would be later, when the ice would grow to several feet thick.

Fort Resolution, 1900

But nothing was more important than the caribou. The trappers were fond of quoting the Indians: "The caribou are like ghosts; they come from nowhere, fill up all the land, then disappear." When they came, the trapper worked hard to put up a store of meat. That done, he was ready for winter, and the main purpose of his trip: trapping the elusive white fox. By then the barrenlands were snow-covered and the lakes were frozen; sled travel was once again possible.

By the time the snow fell in earnest, and stayed, everything was ready. The sled was loaded, the traces laid out, and each harness checked. The dogs, tethered individually along a chain stretched between two trees or stakes, knew immediately what was happening. They strained at their anchors, eager to be on the trail, for there was nothing a dog loved more than to please his master. Gus D'Aoust, one of the best of the barrenland trappers, described his dogs and their relationship.

"I had a lot of respect for my dogs and they had respect for me in return. I would talk to my dogs just as if I was talking to a human, and they would look at me, listen, and wag their tails. They understood me. I treated them well, and they came first. It's true that a man's best friend is his dog. They worked their hearts out for me. I could always depend on them and they would never abandon me if I was in trouble. I put my trust in them."

No dog is more important than the leader. Every trapper has a story about the incredible feats his lead dog performed. Gus D'Aoust remembered his brother Phil's lead dog Whitey ... "It was February. We were coming from the Thelon River, heading south. We figured to get to a camping place that Phil had used two years previously He had left some wood and three tent poles right out on the open tundra and he hadn't been back since.

"When we struck out in the morning, it was snowing and blowing — a real dirty day. We had been travelling for about three to four hours and were depending on the dogs to get there and to find the place. The dogs hadn't been on that trail for over two years. It was an old trapline, right on the open tundra."

D'Aoust was worried that they were expecting too much of Whitey, but suddenly "the lead dog swung to the left and as soon as he got on top of a hill, Phil stopped the dogs and walked to a rock where he pulled out a trap stick and showed it to me. That lead dog had hit the trail right on.

"We were both thinking the same thing, that the old camp site wouldn't be very far away. Pretty soon the dogs stopped. We looked around but we couldn't see anything. There was a big snowdrift and the dogs stopped right there and laid down. We started kicking the snow around and sure enough, there was the split wood and a few tent poles."

More than one trapper owed his life to a good lead dog.

Trapper Gus D'Aoust and his dog-team

Gus D'Aoust was a young man with a dream when he came to the Thelon country in 1930. He spent more than 30 winters alone in the Barrens, "more than any other white man," he claimed. The routine changed a little over the years, especially with the arrival of airplanes in the North, but the trapper's life as Gus D'Aoust knew it belongs to the only time in history when white men — albeit just a few — really lived and worked in the Thelon valley. They were part of the landscape. They depended on the resources of the land. They grew to understand and respect its ways, summer and winter. They knew that land better than anyone has since. They were, simply, a part of "the Country."

The trappers congregated around the east end of Great Slave Lake, at Reliance, during the last weeks of summer. In the early days they had to prepare for the difficult ascent over Pike's Portage, up to the barrenlands. The float-plane changed all that in the mid-thirties. "It used to take us six weeks to portage to our trapline," remembered D'Aoust, but "when we started to fly, it took one and a half hours, a hell of a big difference."

One trapper at a time loaded the airplane with his complete outfit of tents, canoe, traps, toboggan, dogs, fish nets, rifle and ammunition, snowshoes, winter clothing, bedroll, and food, including flour and sugar, coffee and tea, molasses and jam, dried fruit, lard, rolled oats, and other staples. Most food, of course, would come from the land; without that, they could

Gus D'Aoust at his cabin in Snowdrift

not have survived. No sooner did the plane return from ferrying one trapper into his distant cabin, than another was busy loading the plane again for his turn. This went on for a week.

Once in the Country, autumn was a busy time. Winter was only weeks away and, although the fox season did not open until November 1, there was a lot to do, repairing an old cabin or building a new one, cutting firewood, checking over all the trapping equipment and, perhaps most important of all, laying in a supply of meat for themselves and fish for the dogs.

The smart trapper, according to Gus D'Aoust, waited a couple of weeks into November, when the fur was in prime condition. That way, he said, "we got more than double for our furs." By then the ground was hard and snow-covered; the dogs were anxious to run. Each trapper, in his own corner of the vast country stretching from Artillery Lake east across the Thelon valley over to the Dubawnt River, set out his own traplines, guided by a certain knowledge and powerful intuition.

But what is known of the men themselves? Not very much. In the late 1920s there was only a handful: old Klondike Bill, who had come north after gold in '98, and stayed; Claeson, who only travelled alone and caught more wolves than anyone in the Country; Al Greathouse, who turned 70 in 1929 and trapped for several more years on the barrenlands after that; Clark Croft, one of the first to trap right in the Thelon valley; the Peterson brothers, Evan and Martin, big, powerful, and inseparable; Helge Ingstad, a Norwegian in search of adventure, who spent four years in the Country hunting, trapping and travelling with the Chipewyan, the descendants of the Ethen-eldili; Jim Cooley, who is remembered for heading into the Country impeccably dressed in a blue serge suit and grey felt hat; Gene Olsen and his partner Emil Bode, who in 1930 were found murdered in their cabin beside the Mary Frances River, just upstream from where it joins the Thelon; Howard Price, who had his cabin right on the Thelon, at the big bend, downstream from Lynx Lake, and one year caught 400 foxes. And there were others, but no more than a dozen, each of whom was drawn to the Country surrounding the Thelon by some ill-defined but irresistible force.

Helge Ingstad

Helge Ingstad (2nd from left) remembers:
"we rejoice in the summer after a long, tough winter"

When Gus D'Aoust was an old man in his eighties, living in Yellowknife, he could not leave the trapping life behind. "I'm still driving dogs in my sleep," he claimed. "I wish I were still out there." He continued to work with local trappers, grading, bundling and shipping their furs off to auction. Furs, he said, were his life. In January of 1990, at age 93, Gus died. His ashes were scattered over the Country.

5

John Hornby

*He can travel anywhere and has shown unusual endurance
in starvation, both useful qualifications.*

Guy Blanchet, 1924

Of all the trappers, there is only one name that remains well known: John Hornby; his friends called him Jack. With the passage of time, he became a legend of the North.

Born into privileged circumstances, in England in 1880, Hornby first came out to Canada in 1904. He arrived by ship in Halifax where, notably, he paused to visit a first cousin Marguerite, married to an officer in the British Army, Captain W.F. Christian. Just a few years later, after returning to England from this overseas posting, the Christians had a son, Edgar. That little boy, as a young man, would one day go to the Thelon with his Uncle Jack. Meanwhile, Hornby carried on across Canada to Alberta, to the frontier.

At five foot four and 100 pounds, Hornby was a wiry man, with an endurance that was to be both his redemption and his undoing. While in Alberta for the next few years, he learned a lot of the ways of the bush. He is said to have repeatedly demonstrated his physical toughness, on one occasion by running a hundred miles in 24 hours. In some way, those years established a pattern that took him north and into a career of pitting himself against ever more difficult circumstances.

In 1908, he was invited by another British eccentric named Cosmo Melvill to join a trading and trapping expedition headed for Great Bear Lake. They stayed in the area over three winters, but the trading was only partially successful and the hunting was more effort than they had bargained for. When Melvill left to go south in the summer of 1911, Hornby stayed on, his love affair with the northern wilderness — if not a local Dene woman named Arimo — having taken over his mind.

For the next three years, Hornby remained on his own near the shores of Great Bear Lake. He became part of the country, travelling widely, suffering regularly, but somehow always scraping through. Of one occasion at the time he wrote: "I caught a bad chill and nearly died. I indeed had a hard and miserable time but though I was extremely ill, it did not trouble me as I seemed absolutely indifferent whether I lived or died."

His ability to survive remote and unforgiving conditions cannot be questioned. Neither can the early examples of erratic behaviour that would eventually seal his fate. In the summer of 1914, on the banks of the Mackenzie River, he met a man named R.M. Chipman who wrote in his diary:

> On the day the steamer left, I talked with Hornby for about five minutes and during the conversation he told me he had fully decided on each of four separate things — to go up river on the steamer and go outside; to go as far as Fort Norman and to Great Bear Lake for another winter; to go over the Rat and the Bell [Rivers] and down the Yukon; to go to Herschel [Island] with us and either go outside on a whaler or go to the east with us. Six years in the North was quite enough, if not too much, for him.

In the end, he went south. With the outbreak of war, Hornby joined the army, as much for the free trip home to England as for the opportunity to defend the Empire. By October of that year, he was reunited with his parents in England. In April 1915 his unit, the 19th Alberta Dragoons, sailed for France, where Hornby fought as a private in the Battle of Ypres, one of the war's most miserable. Slightly more than a year later, by then promoted to Lieutenant, he fought in the Battle of the Somme, in which more than a million men died — one of the war's most horrid events. Hornby was lucky; he was severely wounded and evacuated. The war, for Hornby, was over: he wore a Military Cross, "for gallantry in the face of the enemy," and bore psychological scars of battle that may provide some explanation of his subsequent actions in the barrenlands. Within two months of his return from France, Hornby was back in Canada. He pined for the North where the wilderness offered the solace he sought.

By late September 1917, Hornby was once again on the north shore of Great Bear Lake. He spent two lonesome winters there, almost starving, before leaving in search of new frontiers. After a year of aimless travel down to Edmonton and back up through Fort Chipewyan to Great Slave Lake, he formulated a plan to once again establish himself as a trapper and trader, this time on Artillery Lake. In mid-September 1920, he arrived at the east end of Great Slave, but was unable to proceed farther.

That winter, he fell to new lows of subsistence and desolation, in his own words "barely existing," reduced to "literally nothing but skin and bone." In early March, he wrote in his diary: "Tonight I shall have to put everything in order, in case anything happens. It is very easy to lie down and give up, but an entirely different matter to bestir oneself and move about." Throughout the winter Hornby had not travelled far afield, had survived on fish and the meagre supplies brought in with him. On one occasion, in March, he "was too feeble to do more than wrap a blanket around his head and crawl on hands and knees to his fishing place almost a mile away." This, in country where the Dene and a few other white trappers enjoyed relative prosperity. He survived, nonetheless, and managed to struggle out to Fort Resolution after the ice broke up.

Here Hornby leaves the first clue of his intention to visit the Thelon, in a letter to his old friend, from Great Bear Lake days, George Douglas: "I should very much like to spend a winter on the Arkilinik [Hanbury's name for the Thelon River], for I am sure that one could

JC Critchell-Bullock

John Hornby, 1923

there get a lot of caribou and fur." He had, apparently, read enough to know Hanbury's name for the river, but not enough to heed Hanbury's wisdom on attempting to pass a winter there.

The pattern continued the next year, with Hornby barely scraping by, and surviving more than his share of close calls. He never learned, it seems, or didn't want to. Unlike every other successful white traveller in the barrenlands, he eschewed preparations. He took pride in an ability to "out-Indian" even the Native people.

During the autumn of 1923, in Edmonton, Hornby met another Englishman, a younger man just out of the British Army now searching after greater adventure, Captain J.C. Critchell-Bullock. Together they began to lay plans for a "scientific expedition" to the country northeast of Great Slave Lake. Critchell-Bullock took the science perhaps more seriously than did Hornby, for whom it might have been little more than a way to get there. They gathered the support of Guy Blanchet, an extremely competent government surveyor, who had been materially assisted by Hornby's knowledge of the country during his previous survey of Great Slave Lake. Blanchet suggested to O.S. Finnie, head of the North-West Territories and Yukon Branch in Ottawa, that Hornby be asked to report his observations — of caribou migrations and of musk-oxen on the upper Thelon — to the Department, and correspondingly be paid a small salary and given rations.

"I think Hornby might be quite good at such work," wrote Blanchet. "He can travel anywhere and has shown unusual endurance in starvation, both useful qualifications."

Hornby went home to England, to visit his ailing parents. While there, he received a letter from Finnie offering an appointment. Hornby cabled his acceptance and sailed from England two days later, on May 30, 1924.

The government assignment, it seems, was secondary to Hornby. By now he felt compelled to write his own account of the Country; he already had something of a rough manuscript entitled *In the Land of Feast or Famine*.[*] Regardless of his true motive, he stated categorically that "this is my last trip to the Arctic." By the end of August, Hornby and Critchell-Bullock were at the east end of Great Slave Lake. With them were several trappers, including Al Greathouse, on his way in to build a cabin beside Artillery Lake. Hornby and his partner went 30 kilometres farther north, beyond the treeline to the barrenlands, to the mouth of the river flowing in from Casba (Ptarmigan) Lake. On a big esker just west of the river, five or six kilometres from Artillery, they prepared to spend the winter.

Digging into the sand and gravel, they created a hole that measured about three metres by two. Using thin spruce boughs, they lined a roof with caribou skins and covered it with

---

The manuscript subsequently disappeared and was never published. Helge Ingstad's book about his years as a trapper was published in English under very nearly the same title – a coincidence, he claimed.

sand. The whole mass was supported by at least 30 upright poles, providing just enough headroom to stand up straight. It was dark and damp, and the sand got into everything, but it was at least some shelter from the winter blasts. In any case, it was to be their base for the next seven months.

There were four other white trappers on the lake that winter: Al Greathouse along with his young partner F.L. Buckley, and the brothers Malcolm and Allan Stewart who over-wintered just east of the Casba River. Hornby was attracted to such company; these men suited his temperament, more so perhaps than did Critchell-Bullock, who at least professed more dedication to the scientific aims of the expedition. Hornby, like the trappers, enjoyed the independence and freedom of the trappers' life. That winter, probably only the third in which the area had been extensively trapped, Greathouse took 137 white foxes, the Stewarts 400, Hornby and Critchell-Bullock a respectable 358. Word of their success spread quickly, and soon other trappers moved up from Great Slave. It was only a matter of time before one of them would venture east into the Thelon valley.

Hornby and Critchell-Bullock passed a miserable winter. Their "house," lit by only one small window, was often unbearably cold, well below freezing. As time passed, it became ever filthier. Fox skins and blood stains were everywhere. Writing of his "most unenviable position" in mid-winter, Critchell-Bullock described conditions from his point of view. "The worst storm of my experience blew for seven days. For three days I was without fuel, and living on raw oatmeal and snow. Everything became frosted up, my beard and the edge of my sleeping bag a mass of ice, underfed, my blood temperature became lowered ..." But perhaps worst of all was the abiding incompatibility of the two men.

In April, as winter neared its end, an RCMP patrol arrived at Artillery Lake by dog-team from Fort Resolution. They checked on the well-being of all the trappers and brought the mail, but paid particular attention to the condition of Hornby and Critchell- Bullock. Rumours abounded that one or the other had gone crazy, dangerously so. Neither had, concluded the RCMP, but the Corporal nevertheless advised Hornby to come out via Great Slave, not to proceed as planned eastward across the barrenlands to Hudson Bay. Less than two weeks later, Hornby wrote to O.S. Finnie, informing his superior in Ottawa that they would be going out via the Thelon, "to study the musk-ox on the way" and expected to arrive in Ottawa by late August.

On 19 May 1925, Hornby and Critchell-Bullock set out from the north end of Artillery Lake. They had more than a ton of gear and fur — including at least $14,000 value in fox and wolf pelts — to transport in their two canoes. But that is only part of the reason why they advanced so slowly. Fifty days later, they were only 130 kilometres from Artillery, having laboured over many portages, lost their way, been delayed by ice conditions and hunger, and being generally disorganized. It was July 19 when they finally reached Helen Falls on the Hanbury, and knew that the portaging was over.

"At this time we were rather under-fed and inclined to take chances," wrote Critchell-Bullock later, omitting the fact that he had just had a narrow escape with his canoe in the rapids above Helen Falls. "Consequently we managed to make a fifty yards portage of Helen's Falls by running down to the brink, and lowering our loads and craft over the precipice immediately below the fall. This was safely accomplished, but lining the canoes down the left hand side of the gorge was, as it happened, far from a simple undertaking. The result was we almost lost the entire contents of one canoe, and our lives, from a landslide that suddenly hurtled down on us from the cliff above."

The worst, however, was over. It was only a short paddle down to the junction with the Thelon proper, and a clear waterway to Baker Lake. Just below the junction, on July 23, the two hungry men saw 2,000 caribou moving upstream along the east bank of the river, "a beautiful sight on the sand hills with the gold of the sunshine reflected on the water of the river." The tracks of caribou are still evident on those sand hills today, and almost every year within a few days of that date, large numbers of the animal move along this stretch of the river.

Perhaps the most significant event of the entire trip took place six days later, when John Hornby was drawn ashore at a sharp double bend in the river to inspect what he called "good spruce timber 10 ins to 15 ins in diameter," suitable for building a winter house. Forgetting his previous conviction that "this is my last trip to the Arctic," he told Critchell-Bullock that this was a place he would like to come back to, to over-winter. He did; his remains are still there. Today we know it as Hornby Point.

———◆———

John Hornby and James Critchell-Bullock, filthy and in tatters, arrived at the Baker Lake trading post on August 27, 1925, a hundred days after they had left the top of Artillery Lake. By a string of vessels — motor-boat, schooner, and steamer — they made their way to St. John's, Newfoundland, then on to Halifax, and eventually by rail to Ottawa. Along the way, they discovered that the pelts carried throughout the journey had been ruined, and were worthless, $14,000 lost. During a brief visit in Nova Scotia, an old friend from Great Bear Lake days asked Hornby if he had kept sufficient notes to satisfy his contract with the government. The reply was characteristic: "Oh No, not one. I never wrote a thing. I'll get some from Bullock ..."

Upon arrival in Ottawa on November 19 — not August as prophesied — Hornby set immediately to work on his fabrication of a report. He was anxious to go home to England. A week later the draft was ready, and a week after that he submitted to O.S. Finnie a document of 16 single-spaced, typed pages, entitled *Report of Explorations in the District between*

Artillery Lake and Chesterfield Inlet. By then he had also delivered to the National Museum more than a dozen specimens, skins and skulls, collected from the barrenlands. His friend there, Dr. R.M. Anderson, head of zoology, later recalled Hornby coming into his office, to "empty mummified and mouldy mice without data out of the pockets of his best suit."

Hornby's report somehow managed to be substantial in its content, presumably the result of what Critchell-Bullock called "his amazing interest in natural history, strikingly manifest in the field." One section, above all, deserves recognition still.

"The results of the trip show that there is a large uninhabited area where musk-ox are plentiful, swans and geese nest and caribou can have their young undisturbed by man. This wooded area possesses no minerals, containing only sandstone and sand, consequently can afford no inducement or excuse for men to go on a prospecting trip. If it is desired to protect the game in this part of the country, it is essential to take measures to prevent traders from encouraging natives to hunt in this district. A few years perhaps and it will be too late." He went on to note the impact on the caribou of encroaching man, commented on many other species, and concluded with the recommendation that "the area adjoining the Hanbury and Thelon Rivers would make an ideal sanctuary and that neither white men nor natives should be permitted to enter."

With the report in, Hornby sailed for England, just in time — his father died on December 17, 1925. Meanwhile, back in Ottawa, his opinion was taken seriously. Finnie had been looking for a way to accomplish this purpose, and saw Hornby's report as the vehicle. He passed it on to the Deputy Minister, who wrote a note in the margin opposite the sanctuary recommendation: "Action taken 9/12/25."

Critchell-Bullock, who cared rather more than Hornby about the means to an end, had by now ensconced himself comfortably in a fashionable part of Ottawa, just a few blocks from the former residence of Prime Minister Wilfred Laurier, now occupied by his successor as Liberal leader, William Lyon Mackenzie King. Critchell-Bullock had his personal letterhead prepared, and was ready to take up an appointment with the Department of the Interior. All in good order, his task was to prepare the detailed report of the journey, for which he was paid $600. It was delivered, finally, on March 22, 1926, adding further fuel, no doubt, to the fire being fanned by Finnie for the establishment of a sanctuary.

Of the trappers who entered the Country, perhaps none was more colourful, more enigmatic, or even more resilient than John Hornby. Certainly none was more erratic. Today he is remembered for the tragedy that — at this point in the story — was yet to befall him. Nonetheless, he is deserving of credit for his role in the creation of the Thelon Game Sanctuary.

The graves of Edgar Christian, John Hornby, and Harold Adlard

6

Legend by Death

To penetrate this country in the dead of winter would be simply to court starvation. Then the deer have all departed, and to depend on finding musk-oxen at the end of the journey would be risky indeed.

David Hanbury, 1899

The barrenland trappers were gathered at Snowdrift early one summer, as usual. One of them asked if anyone had heard or seen anything of Jack Hornby. Helge Ingstad remembers someone commenting, "He's probably done for. He was figgerin' on dying up here in the North." And then old Klondike Bill added, "It was bound to be like that. The Country sooner or later does away with all these fellers that try to act tough." The mystery that surrounded Hornby at that time has grown over the years into a legend. For many people, the last chapter in John Hornby's saga stands as the ultimate testament to the wildness of the Thelon valley, and the ultimate measure of its mysterious allure.

———————◆———————

Not more than a few months after submitting the report that triggered government action to create the Thelon Game Sanctuary — a report based on what he claimed was his "last trip to the Arctic" — John Hornby was making preparations for a return to the Thelon.

Back in England during the winter of 1925/26 he once again made contact with his cousin Marguerite Christian and her family, whom he had last seen in Halifax at the outset of his first trip to Canada. Hornby, at 46, was the same age as Marguerite and Frank Christian. Their young son, Edgar, now 17, had recently finished school. We can only guess at how his youthful imagination soared with his Uncle Jack's tales of the far north. In any case, plans were soon laid for Edgar to accompany Hornby back to Canada's north country. Edgar's father, an army officer, felt it would be an experience for the young lad "to build his life on." Like Hornby himself, they all believed Hornby knew the Thelon country better than any man alive. They could not know the hazardous course that young Edgar was set upon.

Marguerite Christian

Edgar Christian, age 17, 1925

On April 20, 1926, their ship was leaving Liverpool in its wake, bound for Canada and adventures unknown. In Edgar's pocket was a letter from his father saying, in part, "You are out to lay the foundation of your life & all your future depends on how you face the next few years." He could not have known the irony of these words.

On their way across Canada, Hornby and his protege met another young Englishman, 27-year-old Harold Adlard, in Alberta to learn farming the hard way. He had held onto a dream of going north with Hornby for some years since they had first met in 1923; now was his chance. Hornby agreed, thinking the company would be good for Edgar. By the end of May the three were headed north on the Athabasca River by canoe. Their route took them across Lake Athabasca, with a stop at Fort Chipewyan, then down the Slave River to Great Slave Lake.

According to Edgar's own record, they carried with them "a pretty heavy Load for the Canoe... nearly 2000 rounds of Ammunition and traps and a stove and bedding and tent and some grub to Last till the winter comes and then we kill meat which will keep in the snow and ice." By Hornby's previous standards, they were well equiped.

They carried this load over Pike's Portage at the east end of Great Slave, to reach the barrens beside Artillery Lake in early July. En route, they passed some of the barrenland trappers who were headed out of the Country for the summer: Gene Olsen, Al Greathouse, Matt Murphy and others. They were the last to see John Hornby, Edgar Christian and Harold Adlard alive.

Little is known of their trip to the Thelon, except that they travelled slowly. In a cairn beside the upper reaches of the Hanbury, Hornby left a note for some of his trapper friends, the Stewart brothers, which read:

> *About Aug. 5th 1926*
> *Owing to bad weather and laziness,*
> *travelling slowly. One big*
> *migration of caribou passed yesterday.*
> *Hope to see you all soon.*
>
> *J.H.*

Yellowknife Museum Society/NWT Archives

The cabin where the three men spent the winter, as it appeared three years later

Not until early October did they arrive at the sharp double bend in the Thelon River where Hornby had noted, just the year before, a quantity of "good spruce timber" suitable for building a winter house. For Hornby it was the realization of a dream; for Christian and Adlard it was unimagined adventure.

Edgar Christian began his now famous diary on October 14, 1926. By then, there was snow on the ground, the cabin was almost ready for habitation, the men had set out a trapline, and they had a small supply of caribou meat on hand. Prospects for the coming winter must have looked good. Indeed they could have been, but for one insurmountable problem: the three were not to see Hornby's predicted huge herds of migrating caribou anywhere in the vicinity of their cabin. At the very least, that meant a tough winter lay ahead.

The story of that winter comes to us in the form of young Edgar's diary. Without it, the uncertainty of how these men struggled would be sufficient to have relegated them to forgotten history. Edgar's compelling record assured them the immortality of legend.

Oct. 18
Jack returned in the evening with glad news having seen 30 caribou on a distant ridge behind Camp, so tomorrow we all go out in last effort for Winter's grub.

Oct. 19th
We all started out early for to see if caribou were grazing still on ridge behind camp but were soon dissapointed in seeing nothing for miles around and as a strong, cold N.E. wind was blowing and Caribou in any case having no fat on, we decided to turn back and finish fixing up the house. Weather much colder all day but river still flowing.

The first blizzard hit on October 25, and lasted four days. The severity of their condition hit home. They redoubled their efforts to hunt caribou, but there were none to be found. By the end of November, they were surviving largely on ptarmigan and fish. December was a difficult month, but they caught just enough small game to maintain the status quo. Hornby worked prodigiously at hunting, trapping and setting nets through the ice, in a vain attempt to sustain his young charges. The pattern continued through January, with the temperatures dropping into the minus forties, even, on one occasion, down to -54°F. At month's end, Edgar's diary records their situation.

31st January
At last the end of the worst month is over and still grub on hand for 10 days but damned

slim at that. Harold went out and got nose frozen which means denning up more and eating less grub because impossible to go hunting if any danger of freezing. A very cold day.

The next day they sighted caribou, the first in several months. Harold, now strongest of the three, successfully killed one, to provide what seemed a feast. But the feasting was short-lived.

11th February
Hope to God we get Caribou soon as nothing seems to get in traps and flour is nearly gone and we are grovelling round for rotten fish.

16th February
We have 12 cups of flour and 20 lbs of Sugar and hides for food now.

A week later, Harold sighted a band of forty caribou out on the barrens. Hopes soared. All three men went out hunting the next day. Only Harold succeeded; his catch, a young bull, nevertheless provided "an Excellent feed ... the first good meal for Weeks now."

That was their last caribou kill. Although on several occasions they saw tracks, and at least twice spotted the animals at some distance, they had no way of giving chase. One wonders if Hornby, at this point, doubted the wisdom of his foolhardy, but characteristic, decision not to bring dogs and a sled. Without them, hunting was limited to a decreasingly small radius from the cabin. As March passed, the men grew ever weaker. They had abandoned the futile fish nets, and the traps produced only a scant supply of foxes, hares, and birds. They resorted to digging up fish bones and subsisting on boiled animal skins, tossed aside in the more abundant early days at the cabin. Survival hung in a delicate balance. As he had many times before, John Hornby clung to life, against incredible odds. This time, however, the deprivation was too much for him. On April 6, he made his last fruitless outing in search of food. Four days later, lying in pain on his bed, he told the two younger men that he was "sinking fast." Edgar attended to his beloved hero with dedication, but the end soon came.

April 17th
At 6.45 Last Evening Poor Jack passed peacefully away. Until that minute I think I remained the same but then I was a wreck. Harold good pal was a Marvel in Helping me and putting things a little straight for the night. ... Today Harold and I do just the Essentials and I am looking over certain things as well. We both are very weak but more cheery and

determined to pull through and go out to let the World know of the Last days of the finest Man I have Ever known ...

Two days later, Harold Adlard took to his bed, never to rise again. He died on May 4, 18 days after Hornby, leaving the youngest member of the threesome to fend for himself. Hornby and then Adlard, each in turn, wrapped in blankets and canvas, were laid to rest in the snow just outside the cabin. Edgar Christian soldiered on bravely, unable to hunt, relying on what lay under the snow around the cabin.

Today I resumed my digging and again had luck in finding more good food which had been discarded. 1 very fat wolverine gut + kidneys and heart and liver and 1 fox gut. A quantity of meaty bones and enough fish for 1 meal.

The diary entries continue through May, a litany of terse, poignant facts describing his declining condition, always heartened by a slight ray of optimism. On May 18th, he saw three robins and a swan fly over, reassuring him that spring was indeed coming, and with it the caribou. The final entry is a disjointed scrawl.

June 1st
Got out   too weak and all in now. Left Things Late.

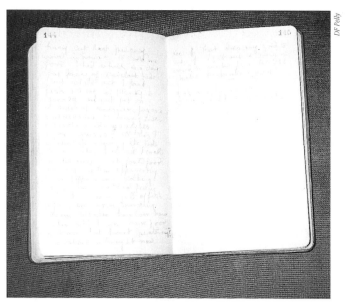

The last entry in Edgar Christian's diary

Those were his final words, written just before the arctic spring would surely have brought relief. He almost made it, but fell tragically short, only a few days before what would have been his 19th birthday in June 1927.

Two weeks after Edgar Christian's last diary entry, the Governor General in Ottawa put his signature on the Order in Council creating the Thelon Game Sanctuary.

———————◆———————

The scene at Hornby Point remained undisturbed as spring turned to summer and the barrenlands surrounding their desolate camp came back to life. Then winter returned, freezing the motionless evidence once again. It was not until slightly more than a year had passed that the next traveller down the Thelon River came upon this grisly sight.

RCMP Archives

The scene at Hornby's cabin as it was first discovered, with two bodies lying to the right of the cabin door

Dr. H.S. Wilson, working for the Nipissing Mining Company, led a prospecting party of four on an expedition to study the area lying west of Hudson Bay. The RCMP had asked them to be on the lookout for John Hornby and his two companions, who had not been seen for almost two years. The prospectors followed the now familiar route north from Edmonton, along Great Slave Lake, over Pike's Portage, and north toward the headwaters of the Hanbury River. On July 21, 1928, they were enjoying a beautiful day paddling down the Thelon, below the junction with the Hanbury. Ken Dewar, a post-graduate student from McGill University was one member of the party. He held memories of that day throughout his life.

"About half way along the grove we spied a log cabin a short distance in from the shore, nestled among the trees. Our first thoughts were that this could be the Hornby cabin, so we came ashore to investigate. There were no immediate signs of life and the place looked as though it had been deserted for some time...

"To the right of the cabin door were two objects all wrapped up, lying on the ground. The one next to the building was first wrapped in burlap and then sewed up in a canvas tarp. The second one was only wrapped in a red Hudson's Bay blanket and tied in places with pieces of small rope. From the shape they appeared to be skeletons with the head next the door. There was one way to be sure of this so I took a knife and made an opening in both objects and revealed the two skulls. They had been dead a long time."

Once inside the cabin, they made note of its contents: table, stove, two watches, a small barometer, binoculars, one trunk and several suitcases including one filled with Hornby's papers, which confirmed their identification, a cooking pot containing some water and the skull of a fox, the only food a half-pound package of tea, a packsack of fur, and three rifles, all loaded.

In the far corners, were two bunks. "The right-hand bunk appeared to have something under the blanket so I gave the blanket a slight pull ... the bones of two feet fell off the foot of the bunk and the skull rolled off to the side," recalled Dewar many years later.

With that, the prospectors had seen enough. The sentiment was unanimous. "We still had a long way to go to a food supply, and also the possibility of an accident was ever present. When Edgar Christian's bones fell off the bed we were of one mind: *Let's get the hell out of here*." They quickly left the cabin and resumed their paddling, taking nothing with them from the cabin. "We put as many miles as we could between us and the cabin before going ashore." They still had many miles to go themselves before reaching the safe end of their journey; the sight at Hornby Point made them deeply mindful of the hazards they faced.

It was now August 1928: somewhat more than a year since the Hornby party had died and, coincidentally, since the Thelon Game Sanctuary had come into existence. In the ironic manner of history, the first warden of the sanctuary, Billy Hoare, was at this same moment descending the upper Hanbury, on his way in to establish a warden's base beside the Thelon, only a few miles upstream from Hornby Point. In that same month, O.S. Finnie, champion of the sanctuary at the Department of the Interior, wrote to the RCMP: "It begins to look very much as if Hornby and his companions have perished somewhere in the vicinity of the Thelon Game Sanctuary." Within a day, Wilson's prospecting party arrived in the RCMP detachment at Chesterfield Inlet on Hudson Bay with confirmation of exactly that suspicion.

Not until the next summer, 1929, was the RCMP able to send a patrol into the Thelon country to confirm the report of Hornby's demise. Inspector Trundle of G Division led a canoe-party from Fort Reliance down the Thelon to investigate. They found everything as it had been reported by the Wilson prospecting party the year before. In the interim, only Billy Hoare and his assistant Jack Knox had visited the site and, ironically, reported evidence of a large migration of caribou passing "within a few feet of the cabin" in early May of that year. It was the RCMP that gathered up the damp papers and a few of the personal belongings, and carefully noted the details of the horrifying scene. The key to today's legend was a single piece of paper, lying atop the stone-cold stove. On it, nearly illegible, were the words WHO ... LOOK IN STOVE. They did, and found Edgar Christian's diary and letters from both him and Hornby. All were preserved from the damaging moisture that pervaded the cabin, thanks (we presume) to Edgar's final thoughtful act: he had placed them in the cold ashes inside the stove. Trundle and his men buried all three corpses and erected crosses over the graves, a few metres from the cabin, and decided to take the diary out with them.[*]

The stove in the cabin where Edgar's diary was found

[*] Edgar Christian's family decided to publish the diary, as Unflinching: A diary of tragic adventure. *Its appearance, eight years later, moved Critchell-Bullock to write Edgar's father – See Appendix V: Letter from J.C. Critchell-Bullock to Colonel W.F. Christian.*

Several years later, Hornby's old friend George Douglas, trying to reconcile the dead man's place in history, wrote: "He made no contribution to the history or to the general knowledge of the country or its inhabitants. To those who really knew him, he was merely the subject of many amusing stories. I can relate many from my own memory. He had many fine traits such as generosity mixed up with most exasperating ones. He often visited us here [Douglas' home near Peterborough, Ont.]: my wife got a lot of amusement & interest out of his visits but he couldn't stand any kind of regularity, method, or order. He was lacking in some of the essential requirements of a good traveller in the North though he was good with dogs. He was no hunter, indifferent fisherman. He was a good walker, runner, or packer. He was good with dogs except in getting something for them to eat by his own unaided efforts. For he was certainly no hunter. He was highly inconsistent and in most things quite unreliable. An important exception was his staying with the job once he got started in the wilds."

Hornby went to the Thelon expecting to find caribou to sustain his party. Having seen how heavily wooded were the riverbanks, he no doubt expected abundant caribou even in winter, for he knew the caribou migrated to the forest edge near Artillery Lake, farther south. It was logical. But it was untested, and it proved to be wrong. So the men starved.

John Hornby had gone into the Country with a plan to write a book, *In The Land of Feast or Famine*. Instead, he gave birth to a legend which will endure as long as people go to the Thelon in search of the mysteries of wilderness.

———◆———

Prior to this fatal trip, Hornby's delicate balance as he teetered between survival and starvation was largely a solo act. This time, a new dimension was added, a complication — two young men for whom he took some responsibility — that tipped the balance fatally. His decline was contributed to in no small way by the efforts he made to get food for the others and, it appears, by depriving himself in order to feed his young cousin. Hornby was, in fact, quite adept in some wilderness skills, and he had shown amazing endurance. On his own at Hornby Point, he might well have survived, to paddle his canoe out to civilization one more time, and his book *In The Land of Feast or Famine* may well have been published.

Since that time, a growing number of canoeists have passed Hornby Point. They almost always stop, walk up the north bank of the river and cast their eyes upon the ruins of the cabin, the axe marks in the trees, and the silent graves. They ask themselves, "Why did he do this? Why did he bring these young men here? What was the draw of the Thelon for John Hornby?"

It is inescapably a moving experience.* Ironically, there are abundant signs of large game frequenting the area: moose, caribou, and musk ox. The grassy layer on top of the graves is enriched by the droppings of ground squirrel, fox and ptarmigan. There is life. Yet there, in the form of three tiny crosses, stands the symbol of death. It strikes deeply because of where it is: in the middle of what remains a wilderness, a sanctuary, an inner sanctum where Man seeks reason.

* *For a complete description of the site, and how to find it, see Appendix IV.*

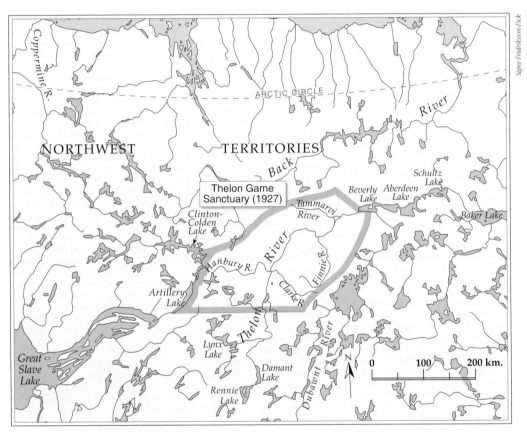

The original boundaries of the Thelon Game Sanctuary as it was established in 1927

7

A Sanctuary created

There still remains, I am happy to say, one spot in this Great Barren North land — which is sacred to the musk-ox — into which human beings dare not enter. Here the animals remain in their primeval state, their solitude undisturbed by the hated sound and sight of man. Long may they remain so.

James Critchell-Bullock, 1925

David Hanbury, 1900

For the preservation of the musk-oxen — which may be so easily slaughtered — and are already rapidly diminishing in numbers, I would suggest that the territory between the Thelon and Back rivers be set apart by the Government as a game preserve.

James W. Tyrrell, 1901

There is a large uninhabited area where musk-ox are plentiful ... If it is desired to protect the game in this part of the country, it is essential to take measures to prevent traders from encouraging natives to hunt in this district... The area adjoining the Hanbury and Thelon Rivers would make an ideal sanctuary.

John Hornby, 1925

I hope that sufficient interest will be aroused permitting work to be carried out on such a scale that that vast arena comprising almost a sixth of the total area of our country may be known and cherished by all Canadians as the world's greatest game sanctuary.

James Critchell-Bullock, 1925

The pressure mounted. Musk-oxen were deemed to be threatened. However, whatever "action" the Deputy Minister of the Interior recorded late in 1925, in his scrawled marginal note on the Hornby report, took a year and a half to bear fruit. The Order in Council establishing the Thelon Game Sanctuary is dated 15 June 1927.[*]

The rationale is clear in the document. "There are only two small herds of muskox left on the mainland" and "there is grave danger of them being exterminated." A game sanctuary comprising some 15,000 square miles (39,000 sq. km.) was "in the interest of conservation of wild life in general and musk-ox in particular." The musk-ox population had been severely depleted by Native hunting to meet the commercial demands of fur traders. The market for musk-ox robes, used in open carriages across southern Canada, grew rapidly in the late 19th and early 20th century, after the decline of the prairie buffalo. In 1917 the purchase of musk-ox skins was prohibited, but it was already too late for most of the musk-oxen. By the time the Thelon Game Sanctuary was created in 1927, the remaining musk-ox population on the mainland counted only a few hundred.

Still, very little was really known about the new sanctuary or about the animals it was designed to protect. A Royal Commission on Reindeer and Musk-oxen was established to determine what measures should be taken. The commissioners, wisely perhaps, decided that not enough information was available, although they did recommend that wolves and "other enemies of caribou" should be exterminated. Ottawa decided to send someone up there to have a good look around and report back on his findings. The Department of the Interior, N.W.T. Bureau, assigned one its toughest, most experienced northern hands: William Henry Beer (Billy) Hoare. Hoare was one of the department's Special Investigators, along with the likes of Dewey Soper and Guy Blanchet. His northern career had begun back in 1914, running the mission boat for the Anglican Church in the western arctic. During those early years he learned to survive in harsh arctic conditions.

Hired by the Department of the Interior in 1924, his first assignment was to conduct some preliminary investigations of the caribou upon which the coastal Inuit near Coppermine were dependent; they were left starving by an unexplained change in the migration patterns. In the next two years, with a single Inuk companion, Hoare travelled more than 3000 kilometres by dog-sled, following the caribou migrations across the barrenlands. He had just completed and submitted his *Report of Investigations Affecting Eskimo and Wild Life, District of Mackenzie, 1924-25-26*, when the Thelon Game Sanctuary was established. In the autumn of 1927, he received his new appointment as the first warden for the Thelon Game Sanctuary.

_____

See Appendix VIII – Order in Council P.C. 1146 dated 15 June 1927

Hoare, age 37 and no newcomer to the North, understood the immensity of his assignment. No longer was the Thelon valley the completely unknown mystery it had been to the few earlier white explorers; yet it still held out the promise of adventure, challenge and uncertainty in a measure which few men sought. Those who did were attracted by more than a sense of duty; something about the Thelon valley drew Hoare to it.

During his careful preparations, Hoare acquired six "thoroughbred Husky sled dogs" from Baffin Island, knowing his life might depend on them. Later, he credited the dogs for their "splendid service" throughout the expedition. The dogs arrived in Ottawa from the North when the grass was still green — Hoare kept them chained to trees in the garden of his Ottawa home, where he lived with his wife and their young family. The dogs needed to get used to one another and, according to Hoare's theory, to fight it out among themselves in order to establish their own leader. He named them Plug, a big heavy dog who became the leader, Nanuk, Cinnamon, Wolf, Silver Tip and Blackie. Unaccustomed to the southern climate and surroundings, the dogs would howl mournfully at night, disturbing Hoare's neighbours. But his control over the dogs was such that the instant he opened the door of his house to come out and quiet them, the howling stopped. He trained them during that fall, never treating them as pets, but teaching them who was boss. When winter came, the local Humane Society insisted that he build six dog-houses, but for these Baffinland huskies the Ottawa winter was mild — they slept draped over the top of their houses so as not to get overheated. Years later, one of Hoare's northern colleagues, Dr. C.H.D. Clarke, recalled that "his handling of a silly Humane Society inspector produced, when told, uproars of laughter in the north."

Setting out from Ottawa together with his dogs in early January of 1928, Hoare followed a route to the trailhead not appreciably different from that of his predecessors, Hanbury, Tyrrell, and Hornby. By now the railway had pushed slightly farther north into the Alberta wilderness, so Hoare was able to disembark at Fort McMurray.

That he embraced his dogs as vital to the collective effort is evident in the opening entry of his journal:

> I had quite a time getting the dogs through the Village as they wanted to go into every yard. Once I got them on the trail they went very well. We took the trail to the Clearwater river and proceeded down it about two miles to its northern junction with the Athabasca River with a load of about 300 lbs. and me riding most of the way .. the dogs went 18 miles to the H.B. [Hudson's Bay Co.] shipyard in 4 hours and 10 minutes.

At this, the beginning of a long journey, Billy Hoare was travelling alone with his dogs. In Fort Smith, a warden with the staff of Wood Buffalo National Park, A.J. "Jack" Knox, met with Hoare and all parties being agreeable, was assigned to join the expedition. What Knox could not know at the time was that his life would revolve around the Thelon for many years to follow.

On February 9, the two men mushed their respective dog-teams into action and headed out toward Great Slave Lake, then east over the snow-packed ice. Hoare complains repeatedly in his journal that Knox's dogs were not standing up to the test in the manner of his apparently superior Baffinland huskies. Stops at posts along the way and bad weather slowed them down, so they did not pull into Reliance, the last outpost of civilization, until March 5. There they found the huge mound of supplies that had been barged ahead during the previous summer, in anticipation of this expedition. Hoare assessed their situation gravely.

We have just over three tons of goods and we will have to travel well over 1000 miles to move it all from here to our proposed base camp near the junction of the Hanbury and Thelon Rivers. Discussed matters with Knox and we have planned to get as much of our oufit as possible over Pike's Portage and then on as far as possible towards the Thelon before breakup .. this will mean relaying the stuff.

It was a massive undertaking. The striking contrast with their immediate predecessor on this route is immediately evident. John Hornby made a habit of entering the Country without enough food to survive, dependent on the land to sustain him. Hoare took no such risk. He was not there to prove anything, rather to do a job. His inventory included hundreds of pounds of pemmican and dried fish, rice, flour, lard, tea, sugar, powdered milk, rifles and ammunition, sleeping sacks, tents and spare tents, primus cooking stoves, a woodstove and chimney pipes, gallons of coal oil and gasoline, an outboard motor and freighter canoe, a vast array of tools for building, plus equipment "odds and ends."

They advanced slowly, making about seven trips back and forth with their heavily loaded sleds, to accomplish every leg of the relay. Crossing to Artillery Lake over the 40 kilometres of Pike's Portage alone consumed more than a month. From there they had to haul the mountain of gear with only one dog team, the other one returning to Fort Smith with an RCMP patrol. Even the remaining Baffin husky dog team was reduced to five dogs, when Cinnamon became ill and ran off, never to be seen again.

Billy Hoare and Jack Knox, ready to depart from Fort Smith, 1928

Moving up frozen Artillery Lake, Hoare saw toboggan trails leading out from the sanctuary, and surmised that someone had been hunting in there. Not far away, he found a band of ten Chipewyan families, the Ethen-eldili, the Caribou-Eaters, the descendants of Thanadelthur's people. According to his journal, he "warned the Indians that they were breaking the law and that the guilty parties, if caught, would be liable to imprisonment."

Billy Hoare, 1930

In the subsequent, official report, with his bias fully apparent, he described the encounter somewhat more judiciously. "The necessity of creating the sanctuary was explained and the question of game conservation discussed. The hunters admitted that it had not been necessary to go into the sanctuary during the past winter as caribou and fur-bearing animals had been plentiful outside the area. They, however, did not wish any area closed to them as, in times of scarcity, when hard pressed for food they considered it their right to hunt anywhere. I pointed out that, given adequate protection, the animals would be bound to increase, not only in the sanctuary, but in the surrounding area, and that chances of hard times would be greater if there was no sanctuary."

As May passed the snow on top of Artillery's ice turned to slush, and progress by sled became increasingly difficult. They had hoped to move all the outfit overland to the headwaters of the Hanbury River by sled, but the advancing spring made that impossible. Now they were faced with the prospect of portaging it themselves. The two men laboured on. Beside Ford Lake, only 20 kilometres east of Artillery Lake, in mid-July, they recognized that their progress was too slow. A large cache of about half the remaining supplies was built into the side of a gravel hill in an effort to lighten the load. Summer was already half over and they had not reached the river that would carry them down to the site of the proposed base camp site.

———◆———

They advanced only slowly, hampered by the heavy load and foul weather. August and then September passed, and still the men were struggling down the Hanbury River. Although there is not a hint of concern in his journal, this circumstance must have worried an experienced northern traveller like Hoare. Freeze-up came. In mid-October, they abandoned their canoe and set out by dog-sled overland from what is now called Hoare Lake toward the Hanbury-Thelon junction.

On October 19, just nine kilometres below the confluence, they reached "a nice bunch of medium sized trees" and made camp. For Billy Hoare this ended a journey by dog sled and canoe that began 269 days earlier in Fort McMurray, Alberta. Stormy weather confirmed that winter had arrived, so there was little time to waste and lots to do. Most of their supplies remained in various caches farther upstream; at least some must be retrieved. Trees needed to be cut and a cabin built. That the men succeeded in all these tasks is a testament to their determination and strength. Their little cabin in the woods we know as Warden's Grove still stands today as something of a reminder.

A month later, on November 22, dangerously short of rations, they decided to leave by sled for Reliance. Blizzard after blizzard nearly finished them, and imposed delays that reduced their food supplies by month's end to "one pound of rice and three pounds of

Portaging to Campbell Lake on the upper Hanbury: the dog-team pulling the sled, loaded with the canoe, across the tundra

Camped in October 1928, ten kilometres above the Hanbury-Thelon junction

buffalo pemmican." Even that was finished before they reached the large cache they had dug into the side of a gravel hill five months earlier.

> *The supplies were found to be in good condition and the cache intact. Flour, butter, tea, sugar and milk furnished what seemed a wonderful banquet to us that night. The famished dogs were given a good feed of cooked rice, lard, and bacon. The poor beasts had given such splendid service under very trying conditions that we felt the best was none too good for them.*

The men probably owed their lives to those dogs. The expedition mushed into Reliance on December 13, where they passed the worst part of winter in relative comfort, as guests of the RCMP. It was during this period that word reached them, and others around Great Slave, of the demise of John Hornby and his two young companions. It must have had a powerful impact on Billy Hoare, knowing he had built his own cabin only a few miles upstream from where the three corpses lay, victims of their incapacity to handle the Thelon's wildness.

On March 4, 1929 they loaded up once again, and headed back to the Thelon. This time, with only four loads to relay on their lone sled, the journey passed more easily. They

Building the storehouse at Warden's Grove, October 1928

reached Warden's Grove on April 17. Along the way, just inside the sanctuary's boundary on Campbell Lake, they met two Chipewyan hunters and Hoare was once again called upon to act the warden.

> *I hastily went out and was just in time to meet them when they stopped, surprised at coming suddenly on our camp. I asked them what they were doing in the sanctuary. One proved to be an Indian who had spent the night of Feb. 25th with us in the police native house at Reliance and the other was his son. I searched their sleds and found a fresh caribou ham and a white fox that was still warm so it probably was killed less than an hour before. They had also a number of traps, some food, and tent and stove and were intending to camp here for the night then go hunting and trapping. I seized the fox as evidence that they were hunting in the Sanctuary as they were about 30 miles inside the nearest boundary. I gave them a good meal then let them keep the caribou meat to get out on. They started back the way they had come.*

After a spring at Warden's Grove, the two men set off down the Thelon by canoe, bound for Baker Lake. Compared with what they had endured, this part of the trip seemed easy. They stopped at Hornby's cabin, becoming the second party, after Wilson's, to examine the morbid scene. By ironic coincidence, they "struck a migration of caribou going south" right past the cabin.

A barrenlands trapper, known as Hjalmar Nelson, was ahead of Hoare and Knox on the river; he had passed their base at Warden's Grove earlier in the summer. There is a certain mystery to the man: his real name was Hjalmar Dale, but for some reason he changed his last name. There are unconfirmed, uncertain rumours about his past, but the only man alive who actually remembers him is a fellow Norwegian, Helge Ingstad, and he has nothing but good things to say. The two spent a year together in the Country; in fact, Ingstad credits Dale as the man who taught him everything he needed to know in order to survive as a trapper. "He was a trapper, yes, but something more," recalls Ingstad. "He was more interested in the land behind the horizon than in money. During the year I lived with him as a trapper, I learned to know Hjalmar as a man of noble character, a philosopher in his way. He was liked by everybody, not least by the Indians, for his friendly behaviour and sparkling spirit. Often he travelled alone with his dogs. When he started on his journey to the Thelon, he told me he intended to stay there during the winter. The following year he would build a canoe of willows covered with canvas and paddle down to Baker Lake. I never met him again. I asked why he changed his name; his answer was that there was another Dale in the Northwest Territories. I said 'What about your reputation as a great traveller associated with your old name?' His answer: 'I will make a new reputation on the new name.'"

There is another version of events that circulated among the old northern hands at the time. It claims that one day Nelson came into the cabin he shared with his fellow Norwegian, and found an open letter sitting there. He read it, even though it was addressed to Ingstad from his family back in Norway, telling him they had investigated this fellow Dale and found that "he was not a suitable person for their son to associate with." Accordingly, Nelson (or Dale) promptly packed up his things and left.

In any case, the fact is he over-wintered alone beside the upper Thelon and built his canoe, using the canvas cariole from his sled and even the hides of his dogs to cover his rough-hewn structure. After break-up, he headed downstream and passed Warden's Grove on July 3. On August 1, Hoare and Knox caught up to Nelson, blocked by ice in Schultz Lake.

WHB Hoare/National Archives of Canada/PA 116275

Jack Knox (left) and Hjalmar Nelson (right) beside Schultz Lake, 1929.
Nelson's canoe, built of willow and canvas, is on the extreme right

About this time, rumours were circulating in Ottawa that Hoare, like Hornby the year before, had been lost to the Thelon wilderness. These were dispelled when the threesome reached the Baker Lake post on August 6, 1929, and Hoare communicated with his superiors in Ottawa.

Some quick decisions about the future supervision of the sanctuary were now made. Jack Knox was ordered to return upstream and continue in the role as warden, "to guard the

***Jack Knox (left) and Hjalmar Nelson (right) outside the Revillon Frères
trading post at Baker Lake, 1929***

southwestern part of the sanctuary against Indian poachers." He needed help for the late
season upstream journey.

"Got Eskimo Telirhuk to assist Knox at $40 per month. Also hired Nelson for $100
to go the 400 miles with him [back to Warden's Grove]," wrote Hoare in his journal.

After fulfilling his obligation, Nelson returned to trapping, somewhere around the
Dubawnt River, based out of Baker Lake for at least the next two years. Some years later he
visited Billy Hoare in Ottawa, where he made arrangements to have his name legally changed
from Dale, and then he returned to the Northwest Territories, eventually to die near Fort
Norman in the Mackenzie valley.

Martha Talerook, an old lady in Qamanittuaq (Baker Lake) today, remembers these
times long ago, even though she was a young girl then. She was named after the man,
Telaruk (or Telirhuk, as Billy Hoare's journal records it), who was hired to assist Knox.
Before the journey, Martha gave him two fox traps as a gift. Telaruk, she remembers, was
known as a good drum dancer. A younger brother went with him, but he drowned
somewhere not far upriver, probably in the rapids below Schultz Lake. That news got back
to the post at Baker Lake. Although the family waited for years, expecting Telaruk to return,

he never did. Martha knows nothing more of what happened to him. He remains a part of the Thelon's enduring mystery.

Knox and Telaruk spent part of the winter at Warden's Grove before moving on to Artillery Lake, just west of the sanctuary. That was Knox's base as warden until 1932. He remained in the Great Slave region for the rest of his life, living alone most of the time, hunting and trapping. He died in 1976 at age 91, in his cabin on an island in Great Slave Lake, somewhere near Snowdrift. Jack Knox was buried in the cemetery at Fort Resolution.

———◆———

Meanwhile, from Baker Lake in 1929, Hoare went south by sea, his clothes in rags, looking the very image of one who had barely survived a barrenlands winter. In fact, he sent word ahead so his wife could meet the ship with a suitcase of fresh clothing for him to put on before appearing in public. He did not stay down south for long. Plans were soon afoot for his return to Baker Lake, to carry supplies up the Thelon and establish a warden's base on the sanctuary's eastern flank, to complement Knox's station to the west. The Thelon had called Hoare back, this time for another adventure, another ordeal, another brush with death.

On June 22, 1930 Hoare left Ottawa by train for Winnipeg then north to Churchill on the new Hudson's Bay Railway. He arrived there on June 30 and immediately set sail on the Schooner Fort York bound for Chesterfield Inlet. From there, together with the new Anglican missionary Reverend W.J.R. James and an RCMP constable, Hoare embarked on a small sloop and headed up the inlet toward Baker Lake, which they reached, after considerable difficulty with ice, on July 22, exactly one month after leaving Ottawa.

He hired "native Sujilo and wife, Ututak" to accompany him up the Thelon and set about preparing for the expedition, aiming to build the new warden's cabin near the eastern boundary of the sanctuary. Once again, he was so heavily burdened as to necessitate relaying load after load of supplies upriver in their two freighter canoes. It was nearly the end of August before the party finally portaged around the last rapid, to reach open water in Schultz Lake. Sujilo, having met up with his wife's family, "decided to go no further with me ... reason seems to be that the native [Telaruk] who went with Knox failed to return and the department did not do anything for the parents of his brother who was drowned." Hoare tried to persuade others to join him, but "they do not wish to adventure into strange country," so he continued on alone. He lost most of his outfit when the smaller canoe, which he was towing, overturned in waves and sent its load of food, ammunition, spare parts and equipment to the bottom. Nevertheless, he pushed on, by now enduring the bitter conditions that September brings.

On September 13, caught by a gale on a small island near the west end of Aberdeen Lake, Hoare assessed his situation. "It now seems late in the season to reach the proposed site of cabin on Thelon and get back before freeze up. I am without proper winter clothing or boots, have no sled [or] harness and only one dog. It seems the height of foolishness to go on alone." Three days later, "still a prisoner on my desert island," Hoare wrote "I will be fortunate now if I get away from here before freeze-up."

He did and despite storms, a failed engine, and ice forming around the shore, he rowed and sailed his way back through the lakes and down the river, to reach Baker Lake post on October 10. He was fortunate it was a late freeze-up that year. Ever determined, he began immediately on a plan to relay supplies upriver during the winter, looking ahead to an earlier start for the next summer.

A trapper, Fred Lind, who had moved over to the Baker Lake area from the upper Thelon, helped out. His main cabin was about 15 miles upriver from Baker Lake — from there he ran traplines over to another cabin on the Dubawnt — so that provided a good staging point for Hoare. But it was hard work.

Dec 5, 1930 ... Freighting from Baker. Started across portage to Linds cabin this AM with small load of Freight .. went about 10 miles in hazy weather with east wind then dropped down a ravine which I could not get back out of so had to follow to the river which I struck below the canyon. Piled rough ice in the canyon made terrible going. I cut a roadway through it for two miles with the axe then had to give it up for the night as dogs were played out and so was I. Ate frozen biscuits and drank coffee from thermos then slept on sled.

After Christmas at the post, including "dinner with all other white men at Anglican mission" and a "feast and dance given to natives," Billy Hoare continued his freighting. In February of 1931, he learned that "there is an Eskimo and a team of dogs coming from Chesterfield for me" and when Alphonse Koelatchiak arrived, Hoare found him "a good man." Together they moved lumber and other supplies by sled, camping out as necessary before returning to the post for another load. In stages, that way, they moved slowly up the lower Thelon. On May 11 he recorded that "all our supplies are now at west end of Schultz Lake ... it has been a slow hard task with half starved and several sick dogs." On June 8, they reached the tiny island in Aberdeen where storms had held Hoare prisoner near the end of last summer, and found "Hjalmar Nelson and a native family camped." Nelson had been trapping around the Dubawnt for two years since helping Knox return to the sanctuary. Now

Hoare hired him again to assist with the freighting of lumber and supplies bound for the mouth of the Thelon at Beverly Lake.

Having decided to build his cabin on the point "right at the mouth of the Thelon" on the east side of the river where it enters Beverly Lake, Hoare cached most of his supplies and continued up against the swift current, in search of logs. The country is barren surrounding that 40 kilometre stretch of fast-moving river, so it was not until he reached the small lake just downstream of the Ursus Islands that Hoare saw any promise of timber. There he found "an unexplored branch of the Thelon" and proceeded up a tributary until they found "some fair looking timber." There was some sign that Inuit had been there before cutting timber. This was almost certainly what is now labelled the Tammarvi River, in Hoare's eye "one of the prettiest spots I've seen in the Territories."

Hoare and Koelatchiak spent several days cutting logs, then tying them together into a raft. They floated back down the Thelon, towing their canoe, sitting, cooking, eating and even sleeping on their raft, until they once again reached Beverly Lake. Construction began immediately on the proposed warden's cabin. Although it was in due course completed, it never actually housed a warden for the Thelon Game Sanctuary. Hoare left some supplies to be cached there, and departed early for Baker Lake, where he arrived on July 22. There his journal ends, leaving some mystery about what happened for the rest of the summer and how the cabin was completed. There is some remnant of it still today beside the mouth of the Thelon at Beverly, lying on the top of the headland. It is now called Hoare Point.

Plans to establish a permanent warden service for the Thelon Game Sanctuary were never realized, perhaps because the government disbanded the Department of the Interior in 1932, shortly after Billy Hoare's last trip.

But what of Hoare's main purpose, investigating the musk-ox population? He had seen several during all the trips back and forth through the western part of the sanctuary. In his official report, he attempted an estimate of the current population.

"One hundred and twenty-six musk-oxen had been seen to date in the sanctuary. Some of them had probably been counted twice, but as ninety-three had been seen at one time on June 26, near the mouth of Hanbury River and, as only four cows with new-born calves were seen, which indicated that the rest of the cows had not returned from their calving grounds, I think that a conservative estimate of the number of musk-oxen in the sanctuary at present would be 250 animals. I am concluding, of course, that the cows are at least equal in number to the bulls and that we did not see quite all of the bulls."

Hoare was convinced by his expedition that the sanctuary was a necessary measure. "There is [now] one region on the Canadian mainland where the musk-ox is expected to survive and, eventually, to restock other areas."

It can fairly be said that these two men, Billy Hoare and Jack Knox, had come within a whisker of losing their lives, of becoming additional victims to the Thelon's wildness and fodder for its legends. Shortly after arriving at Warden's Grove the first time, they nearly starved. Had Hoare not known how to make Inuit clothing from the caribou skins he had saved, they would probably have frozen to death. Preparedness and a tough resolve had carried them through, but in the Thelon country, all the resolve in the world — without proper preparation alongside — may not be enough. John Hornby and Edgar Christian had proved that. Hornby's fate might well have become Hoare's; it did not, and the latter is less well known because of it. Even as these early travellers, dead or alive, passed into history, the secrets they unlocked only increased the allure of the Thelon country for other northern adventurers, yet to come.

We should have gone into the wilderness. That is where healing is, and sanity. When you go into the land, you go into yourself also, in dreams, in memories, in talk with the spirits and the dead. Things get clarified in the wild.

Wayland Drew

Helen Falls, Hanbury River

Caribou trails on a Thelon esker

View toward Warden's Grove, on a hillside, left bank of the Thelon River (both)

Sudeten Lousewort *Pedicularis sudetica*

Labrador Tea
Ledum decumbens

Blue Columbine *Aquilegia brevistyla*

Moss Campion *Silene acaulis*

Arctic Lupine
Lupinus arcticus

Twinflower *Linnaea borealis*

photos : *Laurie M. Pelly*

Thelon Oasis

An old Inuit camp, just downstream of Ursus Islands

The lower Thelon River, in the barrenlands

8

Mushing & Murder in The Country

Archie Larocque, a young Métis from south of Great Slave, heard stories about the men up in the Country and he started dreaming. At 17 he was already a good trapper, in the bush around his Fort Fitzgerald home. What if, he thought, what if he could muster the supplies and the dog team and the knowledge to head northeast toward the Thelon, to try his luck trapping the white fox of the Country? The dream seized hold of him.

It was 1931, or there abouts. Larocque and a partner laid plans to head out to the barrenlands. They got as far as the headwaters of the Thelon River, at Lynx Lake — via 52 portages — and there decided to split.

"We were storm-bound there," he remembers, "and another couple of trappers came, Price and Peterson. We got talking. I told them I want to go down the Thelon. They knew a cabin, over on the sand ridge, and said they'd show me where I could get to that cabin."

Between there and the first portage into the Thelon, Larocque helped his partner get settled and then headed down to join the two old hands. When he arrived at the portage, Price and Peterson had gone on ahead, thinking Larocque was on downriver.

"I could hear them below. So I made that portage and I took after them. It seemed like whenever I hit the top end of a portage, they were leaving the bottom end. A couple of places, I looked and it didn't look too bad, so I ran it. I gained a little. But I guess they'd run it too. I got onto this long lake, and they were just pulling out at the bottom end, for the portage. So I paddled hard, then ran and looked at the rapids, to see if I could run it to catch them. It was impossible — too big. I decided I'd never catch them. So I went back, to an island, and I camped there."

Despite searching on his own, Larocque could not find the cabin. So he cached all his outfit on the island, and headed back upstream, to ask his erstwhile partner, whom he thought would know where to look. For a trapper in the barrenlands in the 1930s, nothing was straightforward, everything took time.

"At the first portage there was a falls, about twelve feet. Going back, I had just the dogs, young dogs, about six months old, and an old leader. So when I got to that portage, I just turned them loose, and grabbed the canoe to carry it across. When I came up to the top, looking down, there was a caribou standing there. But there had been no caribou around! So I let the canoe down nice and easy, and I took a shot at it. Damned if I didn't wound it, and it jumped in the river and started swimming across, with all the young dogs behind it. The old dog, the leader, he didn't chase the caribou. He stayed with me — he was smart.

"I thought, hell, them dogs are going to chase that caribou way back inland. I was kinda worried. The caribou got out on the far bank, ran up the shore with the dogs behind it, then back into the same river, toward me. Fine. I'm waiting, with my rifle. But the old fool caribou decided to die about in the middle of the river. Then the pups caught up to it, and they were trying to crawl on top of the caribou, as it was rolling, heading for the falls. There was nothing I could do.

"I grabbed the canoe and ran like hell again, back over the portage. I got down below the falls. First the old caribou came over, then the pups. I grabbed them and threw them in the canoe. Finally I got all five pups that way. I pulled the caribou ashore and skinned it. I took some meat and went to find my partner. He showed me on a map where a cabin was. I went back down again and I found this one. It was way back off the river, up this draw. Nice cabin though. I stayed there that winter."

Actually Larocque spent most of that winter travelling, all through the country of the upper Thelon. He ran trap lines out from his base in different directions, two days' travel each way. It was a good winter for fox, he remembers.

"We made a living, that's about all. A fox was only $13 then. You had to catch lots to make money. Howard Price was one of the best; he got 400 foxes one year. That was a really good catch. He was a good trapper; go, go, go — that's all he knew. He had good dogs too."

There was only a handful of trappers in the Country at the time. Larocque could name a dozen others, operating over a region so vast they rarely saw one another, though they occasionally crossed trails. They left notes in cabins, and generally kept in touch, but each man lived alone, dependent on his own resources for survival. If their trap line took them into new country, and they needed shelter, they would often just build a new cabin. At one time there must have been tiny cabins scattered all over the Country. It was a tough life, but Larocque insists it was a good life.

Asked to describe how to set a trap, Larocque's eyes glistened and his face gleamed with the memories of being on the trap line. "There's only one way," he said with confidence, "and that's the right way." And then he described in minute detail, as if he had done it just yesterday, the setting of a fox trap. You could see him planting the pole — he called it a toggle — around which he loosely slipped the ring on the end of the chain holding the trap. "That way, when the fox is caught, around and round he goes, never tangles up because that ring is slipping."

You could see him covering the trap: "You hollow out a place for the trap in the mound of snow. Then you look for the right kind of snow, cut a chunk about five inches thick and put that over your trap. Then you start shaving. Shave it right down until you can see blue. Then you gotta make it smooth. You generally try to have your trap a half inch below the crust. If a fox steps on it, he breaks through. It's got to be the right kind of snow, shaved down to about an eighth of an inch thick. That'll work.

"You don't have to worry about finding the traps again. The dogs'll follow the same trail. The dogs'll stop right where you set your trap. Dogs'll never lose a trail. You get a good leader, you got it made. You get caught in a storm, just leave him alone — he'll take you home."

As always, Archie Larocque gave the last word to the dogs.

———◆———

After a couple of winters in the barrenlands, Larocque had had enough. He had a girlfriend down near Rocher (Talston) River, south of Great Slave, and he thought to go down there, get married and trap that area. So he pulled all his outfit out to Snowdrift at the end of the season.

"I was waitin' in Snowdrift for the ice to go. When it did, I figured I should be gettin' loaded up and on my way. But I had lots of time. No rush. So I was gettin' ready, and the police come in from Reliance. Well, I knew the guy, Jim Fabien, from Resolution, who was working for the RCMP at Reliance. They were talkin' and they said to me, what are you gonna do? I said, I'm pulling out, goin' south to trap there in the timber. I'm tired of the barrenlands. The policeman said to me, 'Jim's quitting when we get to Resolution. How'd you like to take over his job?' But I said no, I don't think so.

"Well, he kept after me. And Jim told me I should take the job. But I asked him, what the hell'll I do with my whole outfit here? He said he'd buy it, if I took the job. So I said okay. We agreed on $700 for the whole thing: five dogs, sleigh, five harness, a canoe, kicker, couple of tents, about 200 traps, pots and pans, rifle, everything you needed for a trapline.

"So he loaded all my outfit in the canoe, dogs and everything, and we went to Resolution. When he got off, he had my outfit and I went back to Reliance. I had to give up that girl for a while. But she was still there."

CB Donnelly/National Archives of Canada/PA 20428

The RCMP detachment at Reliance, 1931

That was 1934. He was hired on by the RCMP at Fort Reliance. For the next eight years, he was Special Constable Archie Larocque. During that time he guided the most adventurous and far-reaching patrols ever mounted from that station, checking on the welfare of barrenlands trappers, delivering their mail, protecting the Thelon Game Sanctuary and, once, even pursuing a murder suspect. Years later, when Larocque was 80 years old, he sat in his Fort Smith home regaling me with stories. "The RCMP weren't really looking for anything in particular, just the welfare of the trappers. When those men went up to the Country, there was no radio, no nothing. They never saw nobody all winter. So the RCMP had to bring the mail and make sure that all the trappers were accounted for."

Over the years at Reliance, he served with and guided patrols for a number of different RCMP officers. Most of them, as he remembers, were fine men on the trail. None were finer than Tommy Thompson. Nor were any as difficult as Constable Silver. Today, they both make for good memories.

"Tommy learned right away. He followed you. What you done, he done. He was good. Take his turn on the lead. Kill caribou. He was just like an Indian." Typically, they were out on the trail for 20 days out of the month. Together, they travelled thousands of miles by dog-team, all over the barrenlands.

"One day we were going along and I saw a timber patch on the side of a big hill. I figured, we can go and camp there tonight, and tomorrow we'll hit the [Hanbury-Thelon] junction. We got there, and found a nice little tent, with a frame, and three caribou laying there — right in the heart of the Sanctuary. Now, we didn't go there to catch no damn trapper in the Sanctuary, so if there had been more time, we'd have kept going. But we decided there wasn't time, and hoped that trapper don't come. So we had a nice cup of tea there, and we heard a hell of a racket. That trapper's dogs pulled him right into camp. 'You got me,' he said. It was Howard Price. 'Larocque,' he said, 'I shoulda quit trappin' when you went to work with the police.'

"But we told him we didn't come to look for illegal trappers. Tommy told him, 'forget it, we never saw you.' Price said, 'you guys let me off, and I'll never come back trapping.' 'Oh no', we said, 'we want you to come back trapping.' But sure enough, the next year he quit trapping, and went back to Timmins where he came from."

A couple of years later, the RCMP got a report that some Indians had a musk-ox hide hanging in their cabin up the Snowdrift River. Musk-ox hunting was illegal. Tommy Thompson and Archie Larocque were despatched to investigate. It was summer. They travelled part way by canoe, but in time had to abandon their boat and walk along a sand ridge. Eventually they reached the cabin, found nobody home, and a huge musk-ox hide hanging over a pole inside. They seized the evidence and struggled back to Reliance with the unwelcome burden. Later, three men were apprehended for the crime.

"We took the three Indians to Resolution for trial, for shooting the musk-ox. The judge gave them a month a piece, to be served in Fort Reliance. Well, Tommy gets up and explains we have no cells in Reliance. We didn't want them, the three guys. But that's where they're going to serve their term, so we took them back. We pitched a tent for them beside the office. That was fine. I gave them a little ration every day — a little sugar, a little tea, a little fruit — and I used to take them out in the bush to cut wood for the winter. One day, I come down for breakfast, and Tommy asks, 'did you wake the boys up?' I said 'I hollered at them, but they didn't move.' Tommy said he'd go wake them up. He went out. He come back kinda red, and said, 'those bastards are drunk! All three of them.' I guess these guys saved all their sugar and fruit until they had enough for a brew. No more rations for them. We were glad to get rid of them."

Another time, the Indians came into Reliance with stories of a crazy white man up in the Country. "I knew that guy," remembered Larocque, "known him all my life. We called him Moonshine Bill."

A patrol was readied, with the mission to check on Moonshine Bill and, if he was crazy, to take him in to Fort Smith. "Jeez, I wanted to go to Smith in the worst way, you know. I was wishing he was crazy, but I didn't think so." When they arrived on the hilltop overlooking Moonshine Bill's cabin, near the upper Thelon, they saw smoke curling out into the winter air. The police officers pondered how they had best approach this reportedly crazy man.

"We got in there and he was so gol-darned glad to see us, jumpin' around. We stayed three days with him. He wouldn't let us go! Nothing crazy about him." It turned out that every time the Indians moved in on old Moonshine Bill, the only way he could get rid of them was to act crazy. "He was completely normal — crazy like a fox!"

———◆———

Together with Corporal Tommy Thompson, Special Constable Archie Larocque did the most famous of all the patrols through the Country, visiting all the trappers over a 30-day period, looking for clues to the whereabouts of a murder suspect. The murderer was never apprehended, but Larocque claims he has a pretty good idea what happened.

Back in the fall of 1931, the trapper Howard Price headed for a spot near the upper Thelon, where he planned to build a cabin. He passed nearby another cabin on the north side of the small tributary called Mary Frances River and something struck him as strange, even from a distance. He went closer. Lying on the ground outside the cabin were the skeletons of seven dogs, still staked out along their chain. Another team's chain lay empty. Furs, some rotting, were strewn about everywhere. The cabin door was open. He went inside. It was a grisly sight. On each bunk lay the skeleton of a man, only partially covered. Price knew immediately whose cabin it was, but he could not readily recognize his friends. Gene Olsen's skull had been slashed with an axe and several of his ribs had been broken in two. Emil Bode's face had been smashed in completely, presumably with the butt of an axe. Price found a book on the floor. It was Gene Olsen's diary, which he kept regularly. The last entry was dated November 6th, 1930. It read: "We found Telaruk today."

Howard Price sent word through the trappers' network, passed on from one to the next, all the way back to the RCMP at Reliance. In January 1932, now more than a year since the diary entry and a few months since Price's discovery, the police patrol headed out of Reliance bound for the Country, to investigate the reported murder. They found the cabin just as Price had reported, and determined that the only things missing were a Winchester rifle, some ammunition and one dog team. In their opinion, the two victims had been taken by surprise. Whoever had murdered the trappers was a self-sufficient traveller. But he was never found.

The police blamed the missing man, Telaruk. Not everyone agreed. "I still don't know why they blamed him," appealed Gus D'Aoust in his later years. "They had nothing on him. I don't believe that Telaruk was responsible for those murders." Some thought it might have been another trapper, seeking revenge for some unknown wrong.

But popular opinion was with the RCMP on this one. According to Archie Larocque, "a trapper would never murder another trapper — they were all friends. I guess Olsen was on his trap line, found the Eskimo and took him home. Then he killed them while they were sleeping, knifed them and axed them. He never gave them two trappers a chance."

Some years later, the mystery remained unsolved. Early in 1939, orders came into the Reliance post to mount a patrol and search the Country for any sign of Telaruk. There was some thought that perhaps he was living in Knox and Hoare's cabin at Warden's Grove. Corporal Tommy Thompson and Special Constable Archie Larocque were assigned, and preparations began. It was the longest and farthest ranging patrol ever mounted from Reliance into the barrenlands.

On two sleds, each pulled by a team of six dogs, they loaded all their gear: a four-pound silk tent with three dried spruce poles, a Primus stove with kerosene for cooking, a small wood stove for heat, pots, pans, clothing and lots of food. "It was my job," recalled Larocque, "to make sure there was enough bannock. I'd make a sack full of little bannocks. Then I'd cook a great big pot of baked beans. We made a square board frame with a heavy screen, and we'd dump the beans on that, and two men would shake it out at forty below. Pretty soon they were just like marbles. Then we'd put them in a sack. So when you camped at night, you just put a handful into the frying pan. If you had them in blocks, it'd take a long time to thaw out. But they were just like loose marbles. We had everything: mashed potatoes in patties, and caribou meat all sliced. We didn't have to worry. We got along good. We made sure we had lots of grub."

The two men rode their sleds out of Reliance at daybreak on March 1, up over Pike's Portage and across Artillery Lake. That night they made camp on Crystal Island, where they spent the next 48 hours waiting out an arctic blizzard. When fair weather returned they headed north to Ptarmigan Lake, where they stayed with Jack Knox, who by that time had returned to life as a trapper. From him they heard his account of Telaruk.

The story actually began at Baker Lake, when Jack Knox headed back upstream to resume his duties as a warden for the Thelon Game Sanctuary. Knox and Telaruk made their way up the Thelon, stopping enroute at the cabin used with Hoare the previous year in Warden's Grove, then pushing on all the way to Artillery Lake. There, on Crystal Island, they built a cabin for the winter. That was to be Jack Knox's base for some years to come. What, if anything, happened that winter is unknown. But the next spring, Telaruk disappeared. Knox was not, in fact, surprised, figuring "the Eskimo just wanted to go back to Baker Lake." He took only a frying pan, a kettle, a rifle and the clothes on his back — no dogs or sled. There was nothing Knox could do about it, so he carried on with his duties, thinking no more about Telaruk's disappearance. But "the Eskimo" never showed up at Baker Lake. So the police were determined to investigate his disappearance.

———◆———

Tommy Thompson, now in his eighties and living in northern Alberta, remembers the next part of that famous patrol vividly, as one of the finest experiences of his life. "We had no reliable maps of this area, and were dependent on Larocque's instincts and knowledge of Barrens travel to guide us in the right direction. Larocque was the best Barrens traveller in the north country. Without him, this patrol would never have been possible."

They continued into unknown country near the Hanbury River. They were down to the last ration of dog-food, their clothes were wet, and they could find neither caribou nor wood for a fire. The situation was grim.

"So I told Tommy," recalled Larocque, "I'll take six of the best dogs, that's not crippled from travelling, and I'll go find some caribou. I went back half a day and killed three caribou. I've often thought, I could've lost Tommy there — I didn't know the Country, there was no maps, and you don't see your trail very good. If you lose it, you can't find it. But nothing happened; I got three caribou and went back to camp. From there, we kept going. We knew we were coming to the Thelon/Hanbury junction."

They were headed for the cabin at Warden's Grove, uncertain if they would find any clues to the whereabouts of Telaruk, or the man himself, dead or alive. Thompson remembers that "we examined the cabin and surrounding area, but found no trace of Telaruk. It was evident that this cabin had not been used for years."

On their way back to Reliance, the patrol headed south of the sanctuary through the Country where the trappers operated. They spent several days visiting with Howard Price and Gus D'Aoust along their route, discussing further the strange murders which happened more than eight years before but still occupied the minds of those living in the Country. In the end, back at Reliance after more than 30 days on the trail, the patrol had only one new clue to shed light on the mystery. The last person to see Telaruk alive, not long after the murdered trappers had been discovered, was the trapper Evan Peterson. Archie Larocque recalled his account.

"Evan said he was travelling along his trap line one day, farther down to the southeast, and he saw a miserable little snowhouse off the trail about a hundred feet, with a caribou laying in front of it. So he went over and crawled in. The Eskimo [Telaruk] was in there. Evan saw the gun that belonged to Gene Olsen. The Eskimo had it." Larocque paused. This point seemed conclusive to him. Then he continued, with the account according to Evan Peterson. "He was trying to talk to the Eskimo, who talked a little bit of

English. He pulled out his knife because he was going to have a smoke. The Eskimo grabbed his big snow-knife. Evan started cutting tobacco, filled his pipe, and handed the plug to the Eskimo. He cut some for himself and layed his snow-knife down."

Apparently, Telaruk was quite nervous during this encounter. He was never seen again. Evan Peterson said he checked the snowhouse on his next trip along the trap line, but there was no sign of anybody. Years later, Larocque still had his suspicions about what really happened during that encounter, so he asked Peterson.

"One time when we were drinking, I asked Evan if he had killed that Eskimo. He just smiled. He wouldn't say Yes or No. I think he did, because that Eskimo was never heard from. That was the last time anybody ever saw him."

Maybe Archie Larocque was right, maybe not. Perhaps northern justice had its way. No one will ever know for sure. We do know that Telaruk's body was never found. The mysterious murders of Gene Olsen and Emil Bode remain unsolved to this day.

When Tommy Thompson left to go to a new posting, Larocque couldn't imagine working with anyone else, so he headed back to his home territory. But his "retirement" didn't last long. In 1941 a couple of greenhorns — Constables Silver and Brown — arrived in Resolution bound to take over the post at Reliance. Larocque was talked into helping them out. Even on the boat-trip out to Reliance, however, there was trouble. Larocque knew the channels in Great Slave Lake as well as anyone by this time. But Silver was determined to exercise his command, ordering Larocque to steer this way and that. "I knew damn well I wouldn't last with him."

With an introduction like that, it seems little wonder that Larocque did not hold much hope for a happy year at Reliance. He shakes his head in amused despair, even today, at the mere thought of the unusual things Silver did. Such as his decision to stop hunting caribou for dog-food and feed them a mix of corn meal and fat instead.

"Silver figured we could patrol, carrying a big pot of dog-feed and cook it in the tent at night. He was crazy! I told him, 'Silver, if you ever go in the barrenlands with me, you'll never come out.' I didn't mean it, but it worked. He never made one trip with me in the barrenlands. That's what I wanted.

"He wouldn't allow us to use a dog-whip. I asked him, 'are you going to buy whips for Brown and me?' 'No whips on patrol,' he said. Well, there's no gol-darned dog gonna tell me what to do, so when I got to Snowdrift I bought a whip for $12. Silver said, 'well, you might buy a whip, but you'll not be using it.'

"Me and Brown went out on patrol. I told Brown to take his turn on the lead, to give my dogs a little breather. He was good stuff. So he takes the lead and he yells his head off at the dogs, just plodding along. 'How long are they gonna keep this up?' he asked. As long as you let 'em, I told him. 'Give me that whip,' says Brown. I gave it to him, and well, he was a farm boy, eh, so he could use that whip alright. I had a hell of a time to keep up with him. Now he was mad at Silver too."

Later that winter the officer commanding the Division came to visit Fort Reliance. When he asked for complaints, Larocque told him about the whip. According to Larocque, the senior officer turned to Silver and spoke sternly.

"Constable Silver, I'm giving you orders right now to make out an order to purchase two whips, to be used on patrol at *all* times. Patrols are not to leave the post without a whip for each dog-team. And give Larocque back the $12 he paid for his whip."

"So I got my money back," smiles Larocque. "Silver was mad, but I got even with him."

Nonetheless, Larocque had had enough. He told them he was leaving at the end of March. On April 1, 1942, he loaded a sled with all his belongings — "so high the wife had to straddle it like a horse" — and headed out of Reliance for the last time, bound for timber country around Rocher (Talston) River. There he returned to trapping. But he's never lost touch with his old pal, Tommy Thompson. Together, to this day, they re-live the adventures of the patrols they shared in the 1930s. The Country, its dreams and its mysteries have a hold on them still.

9

Qamanittuaq

When Hanbury, Tyrrell and Pelletier passed through Baker Lake, which connects the Thelon River to Chesterfield Inlet and Hudson Bay, the shores were occupied only by scattered Inuit camps. It was not until the summer of 1916 that the permanent presence of white men began, with the Hudson's Bay Company's establishment of a post on Ookpiktuyuk, an island in Baker Lake near the mouth of the Kazan River. Ten years later that post was shifted to the present townsite at Qamanittuaq, "where the river widens into a lake."

There had been some thought to open a post even farther up the Thelon. In a letter dated May 26, 1925 to the HBC Fur Trade Commissioner in Winnipeg, Captain Edmund Mack of the Chesterfield Section wrote: "... having been held up by bad weather for three days, Mr. Mitchell, Sergt. Clay of the R.C.M. Police and myself with two natives, left the Baker Lake Post for the mouth of the Thelon River, at which place we camped for the night. Progress up the river was made by a small 3 1/2 H.P. motor and Sergt. Clay and myself walked up the left bank until in sight of Schultz Lake. I have no doubt whatsoever that with a powerful river motor boat and scows that goods could easily be taken to Schultz Lake and from thence, of course, easily to the Upper Thelon River.

"... From what I have seen, I am firmly convinced that should the Company desire at any time to open up the country West and South-West of Baker Lake, a good route inland with ordinary river transport is available."

No post farther inland was ever established, however, so the Baker Lake post served a vast area of the barrenlands to the south, west, and north. It became the natural centre for the people often called the Caribou Inuit, the "People of the Deer."

Inuit boys at Aberdeen Lake, 1930

Inuit women near Qamanittuaq, 1926

LT Burwash/National Archives of Canada/PA 99426

Inuit hunters near Qamanittuaq, 1926

WHB Hoare/National Archives of Canada/PA 102616

Inuit family at Schultz Lake, 1929

In the typical pattern of the North, close behind the traders came the police and the missionaries. In 1927 both the Roman Catholics and the Anglicans established their missions, and in their competitive way, began to gather local Inuit into their respective flocks. The Anglicans, it seems, won this campaign, but it was a well-fought battle!

Rev. P.B. (Ben) Smyth, the Anglican, arrived first. When Father Rio, the Oblate missionary, arrived a few weeks later to start building the RC mission, he complained — as a fellow Oblate put it — that Smyth had "claimed the whole territory for himself, with the support of the trading company, Anglican in its history and its origin."

During that first winter, Smyth reported an average of about 20 at his services, "largely representing the attendance of the Eskimo resident in the settlement." He did little travel, none far afield, "as dogs are very scarce in this district," although his preoccupation in most letters with the fiercely cold weather might offer a clue as to the real reason. He did recruit a catechist, or assistant, and after a year and half in Baker Lake wrote back to his superiors that "Tapatai is coming along very well. Of course, he is a pagan and some time must necessarily elapse before he has a grip of things."

Smyth stayed only three years. When Billy Hoare travelled up to Baker Lake from Churchill by boat in 1930, he recorded in his journal the presence of a fellow passenger: the new Anglican missionary, Rev. W.J.R. James. James stayed in Baker Lake for 34 years and is remembered fondly still today. That first summer he and his catechist, Thomas Tapatai, built the first St. Aidan's church, which stands today as one of Baker Lake's most historically interesting buildings. Tapatai helped James in his ministry to Inuit all over the surrounding country. "I contact tribes from a radius of about 200 miles in every direction," wrote James. Hoare mentions James' trips up the Thelon during that first winter and it was in the small Anglican mission house that the tiny collection of white men celebrated Christmas that year. At the time, only those few Inuit associated in some way with either the church, the traders, or the police, actually lived at Qamanittuaq. Nevertheless, wrote James, "we have two services in our little Church on Sundays and two in the week. I have almost a hundred per cent at all services. The services, of course, are held in the Eskimo language and the service books are written in the Eskimo syllabics."

His success grew with time. "During my first five years in the Arctic," he reported after 24 years, "I baptised nine Eskimo. Since that time I have baptised 388 Eskimo. These figures should speak for themselves." By that time, 1954, James claimed to have made contact with about 450 Inuit in the region, of whom about 70 were then living close to the growing settlement at the Baker Lake post. But James' real mark of success was that "their morals have been greatly improved. Polygamy and adultery, which was very prevalent among

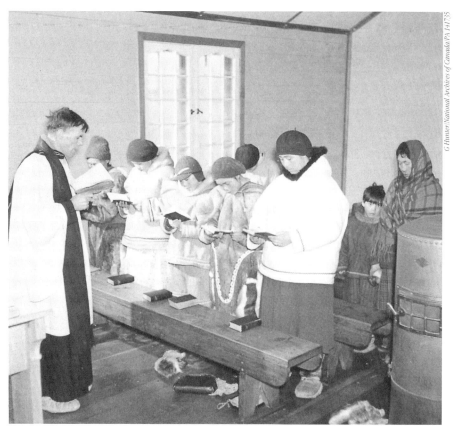

Rev. James conducting a service at Qamanittuaq, March 1946

the Eskimo, is now much less frequent, and magic as practised by the medicine men is now a thing of the past in our district."

This same man was described by a Roman Catholic rival as "filled with anti-Catholic prejudice." Father Buliard, who arrived at St. Paul's RC mission in 1944 (by dog-sled from Repulse Bay, no less), reported to his superiors that if he could not avoid an encounter with Rev. James, it was their habit to "greet each other, but coldly, exchanging a few words in Inuktitut, the only tongue [they had] in common." Father Buliard set about to win back the souls gathered by Rev. James. But a year later he wrote (in French) to his bishop, "Baker Lake is a Protestant stronghold vehemently roused against us with every conversion," accusing the Anglicans of spying and spreading false rumours.

For a short period, the Thelon and the Kazan were Father Buliard's assigned territory. In the spring of 1945, Buliard made his first trip up the Thelon by dog-sled, in search of conversions. On September 18, 1947 he was flown into a camp on Beverly Lake by the legendary RC mission plane, *Arctic Wings*. Later, as winter was settling in, Buliard wrote to his mentor at the mission in Baker Lake, reporting on his contact with the few Inuit he found living this far up the Thelon River, one of whom was "rather ill-at-ease, since he was living with the wife of his friend."

A fellow Oblate recorded the event: "Father Buliard did not hesitate. Such a sinful situation had to be corrected instantly. He ordered the guilty man to fetch his legitimate wife, who lived at the other end of the lake. He had to go at once, taking advantage of a favourable wind. It did not matter that the caribou had just arrived close to the camp; better to die of hunger than to live in the state of mortal sin!"

Father Buliard spent that winter, 1947-48, with the Akilingmiut, the people of the Thelon, around Beverly and Aberdeen Lakes. There were apparently only a few camps in the area. There is only a scant record of his activity, but at least one conversion was recorded by a later Oblate, Father Charles Choque, in a biography of Father Buliard.

"Quite often, he entered a tiny tent, black with smoke, in which the mother of the 'Little Awkward Old Man' lived a life of solitude and misery. She was but a shadow of her former self, always in bed and eaten alive by enormous lice. She thought herself useless, so worn out that she could no longer walk. From her greasy garments, badly patched, exuded a sickening odour; from her torn sleeves her skeleton hands showed ancient tattoos hidden under the filth, her nails as long as claws. Her teeth, worn from chewing skins and tearing away at raw meat, were now nothing but hideous black stumps, no longer able to chew anything. Badly combed, she inspired fear. Father Buliard was heartbroken to see her so abandoned. He brought her tea and biscuits. Little by little, alone with her, at the risk of sharing her lice, he got to speak to her of the Lord. 'I am much too old to understand such things,' she answered him. One day when Father asked her if she wanted to go to heaven, the place of happiness, she replied: 'Yes, if there is neither darkness nor lice.' She was baptized."

As Father Buliard himself said, "I do what I can, I pray, I set good example, I am kind to everybody; I visit often, on occasion I say a word about religion." During his winter on the Thelon, he also travelled by sled up to the Back River, where there were at least more Roman Catholics for him to serve. A few months later he was on his way home to France on leave for the summer of 1948.

After that the missionaries, both Anglican and Catholic, stayed put in Baker Lake more than they travelled the region, as did the traders. Only the Police made patrols around the camps, to take an occasional census of the Inuit, to issue them all with official numbers in the 1950s, and to make sure they obeyed the ban on hunting in the Thelon Game Sanctuary.

According to John Pudnak in Qamanittuaq, "after the Game Sanctuary was established ... in the thirties, even into the forties, people were not aware of the fact ... and therefore people always lived and hunted in that area until probably the early fifties when people found out there had been a Game Sanctuary established.

"... But I think once people were given the proper explanation as to why it was established, then they respected the fact that you couldn't go into the Thelon Game Sanctuary to hunt caribou."

For Silas Putumiraqtuq, a respected elder in Qamanittuaq, it was not so straightforward. He remembered knowing about the game sanctuary even as a young man, but said "that area was one of the best muskox hunting areas," and admitted "my father and my family used to go up there to hunt muskox all the time. There were no other places where you could get muskox."

This sort of tresspass, it seems, was tolerated, even overlooked. When Thomas Qaqimat, as a young man in his mid-twenties, asked the Baker Lake RCMP constable if he could go into the sanctuary to trap foxes in the mid 1950s, he remembers a curious response. "The request could not be approved in particular, but they made it clear to me that it did not make all that much difference to them if I did go in there, because I had to make a living from trapping. I was not requesting permission to go in and hunt muskox or caribou or to fish or anything; I wanted to trap foxes."

Elmer Harp

The creation of the game sanctuary in 1927 occured before most Inuit (or Dene) who used the Thelon valley had more than infrequent (if any) contact with white men. That some remote government, acting far beyond the Inuit horizon, could suddenly designate a portion of their hunting territory as a sanctuary — where hunting and trapping were forbidden — would quite understandably have been inconceivable to the people who lived there.

Life for most Inuit of the lower Thelon valley remained a semi-nomadic cycle of hunting and fishing until quite recently. Small bands of Inuit, perhaps as many as five related families, moved seasonally between summer caribou crossings and winter camps, located near good fishing waters.

Inuit woman beside the lower Thelon, 1958

In the late 1940s, Hugh Tulurialik, an Inuk who now lives in the community of Qamanittuaq, was just a little boy. His family was camped at Schultz Lake: his parents, his grandmother, an uncle and his wife, and young Tulurialik. Food was growing scarce, as they had run out of meat from last fall's hunt. He remembers it well, though at the time he probably did not realize how tenuous was their hold on life.

We moved because there were no caribou and not very good fishing where we were. We were following another family and were behind them maybe two days. They knew the way to go to a good fishing place. I do not think my uncle or my father knew exactly about this place. So we were following their tracks. It was not too cold, but snowing.

I do not know how many dogs we had, something like four or five, enough to pull the sled easily. Before we reached there, two or three of our dogs died of hunger. We kept following the tracks.

Finally we reached the family at their new camp beside another lake [after walking about 250km.]. They were only two days ahead of us but they already had lots of fish. I was cold and hungry, but they just let me have a little bit of fish, because they did not want to feed me too much. I had been hungry for at least three days, about a week maybe. They put me in bed right away because I was cold.

Very early next morning, when everyone was sleeping, my grandmother woke me up and told me to do some fishing. I got dressed, went on the ice not far, and started fishing. As soon as the hook went into the water in the hole, a fish bit it. I took it up to my grandmother right away. Then I went back to the hole. I caught another fish and took it up. Then back down again. I went back and forth, with one fish each time, because I was a child.

When everybody got up that morning of our first day in the new camp, there were lots and lots of fish. I remember that well!

In the 1950s, as in the 1920s and no doubt many times before that, there was widespread starvation. It seemed the caribou did not come. Many people died. Most of those who survived became increasingly dependent on the support offered in the growing settlement of Baker Lake. To meet these needs, the federal government sent the first teachers, administrators and nurses north. The community grew and eventually the government started building small "matchbox" frame houses. By the late 1960s, all of the Caribou Inuit had moved off the land into one settlement or another.

Today, at the mouth of the Thelon River on Baker Lake, Qamanittuaq is a thriving settlement of about 1,300 people. The Thelon remains part of the community's life, regularly drawing people upriver as far as Schultz Lake for fishing and hunting. Most often they travel in 20-foot and larger freighter canoes powered by outboard motors or by snowmobile in winter. Travel beyond Kaninguaq, their name for the lower river, even as far upstream as Tivialik (Beverly Lake), is rare. But the Thelon valley remains very much a part of their mental map. It is spoken of with a certain reverence, of the sort used for important places.

As Barnabus Piryuaq, another Qamanittuaq elder, said: "People have always lived on the Thelon River."

DF Pelly

Barnabus Piryuaq, 1984

A musk-ox bull browsing beside the Thelon River

10

The Biologists

It was July 21, 1991. We were camped not far below Lookout Point. After a day of napping, eating, reading, washing and fishing — all punctuated by occasional rain showers — we left camp to resume paddling late in the day. It was a dramatic evening, with billowing clouds and soft golden light. Not a half hour into the paddle, the spectacle began.

A powerful looking white wolf, loping along the left bank, stopped briefly for a look at us as we slid by silently only metres offshore, and then hustled into the surrounding willow thicket. Seconds later a young bull moose emerged from the scrub brush on the same bank, stood on the gravel beach, spied us and retreated. Not a moment after that we heard a splash a short distance back upstream, behind us, and turned to see a caribou dashing into the water with the wolf just at his heels. As the caribou swam swiftly out into the river, the wolf stopped on the beach and watched his prey escaping. Our thoughts turned to the moose, hoping he was not heading toward the wolf. We need not have worried — just then the moose reappeared on the beach abeam our canoe and this time overcame his uncertainty about us, perhaps brazened by knowledge of the wolf. The moose entered the water and swam across the river past our canoe, leaving the wolf alone on the riverbank. At one point, we could see all three: wolf, caribou and moose!

In the next hour we passed several musk-oxen sleeping peacefully among the willows on the riverbank. Serenity settled into the Thelon valley beneath the amber light of late evening. We had been paddling now for about three hours, and the onset of a night-time chill set us to looking for a campsite. Just as we rounded a sharp bend where the river turns briefly south, there on the point were two arctic terns swooping and diving with all the ferocity they could muster directly over another wolf, this one greyer and smaller. The wolf, we surmised, had come too close to the terns' nest for their liking. To us it looked as if the terns actually hit the wolf on the head during their angry attacks, accompanied throughout by loud squawking. Even though the grey wolf spied us, a distraction to his quest for food, he just continued along the beach, in no apparent hurry to abandon the prospect of a meal. In the end, he did, disappearing up onto the open tundra, without having succeeded in robbing the terns' nest. Shortly thereafter, we made camp on the same bank.

The next morning, just five minutes farther downstream, we stopped on an island where we spotted another tern sitting on her nest. Even as we approached, she remained in position, squawking loudly. Not until we were only a few metres distant did she suddenly rise to begin her mock attack at our heads, hovering just inches away in a fury of wing-beating and panicked crying. There on the ground, in no more than the natural hollow among several cobbles, was a downy nestling, the tern's only offspring for the year, whom she was so anxious to protect. We retreated immediately to our canoe and pushed off.

It was a pleasant day for paddling: warm sun, a gentle wind to keep the bugs at bay, and a favourable current. Late in the morning, at the end of a long, straight stretch of river, we saw more musk-oxen. A herd of 17 — all ages, both sexes, including two new-born calves looking like Bouvier dogs — browsed in the willows right beside the river. They looked up from their meal and gaped as we drifted past, but remained in place, and soon returned to eating.

A few hundred metres downriver, we stopped on the opposite shore for a break. As we rested, stretched our legs, and dipped into the gorp bag, glancing occasionally back up at the musk-ox herd, a lone caribou bull approached the river just upstream of where we stood, entered the water and swam swiftly, assuredly across the river. After ten minutes' stop to graze on the far bank, he climbed to the ridge above the river, until his antlers stood out in silhouette against the clear blue sky. We watched throughout, then turned back to our canoe, ready to depart. There, in front of us, just downstream, was a line of caribou stretching across the river, up the far sloping bank, along the rocky ridge and into the hills. A part of the Beverly herd was crossing right before our eyes, the familiar "river of caribou" image coming immediately to mind, for they seem to flow across the ground as a mass of brown and tawny hues. This herd was a mix of bulls, cows, yearlings and new-born calves, all reunited now that spring calving was over, wandering the barrens in search of food and respite from the bugs. We stood and watched, crossed the river, stood up on the ridge to view even more, never tiring of the spectacle. When finally we left that spot, and continued on our way, there were more caribou, stragglers from the main herd, everywhere along the bank, running aimlessly about trying in vain to escape the black flies.

A red-throated loon, swimming idly in the calm shallows near the shore, looked up at our passing, showed off his brilliant red throat in the mid-day sun, turned his slate-grey head to and fro as if to permit our inspection, then dove elusively out of sight.

We lunched in the canoe, drifting onward with the current between sandy banks topped with willow scrub. Terns swooped down low to the water on either side in an interminable search for food that provided us with an aerial display of precision flying to match any hi-tech fighter jet ensemble. A tundra swan circled in a quiet backwater, its neck outstretched, its head peering beneath the water's surface. Musk-oxen here and there, some as small to our eyes as tiny chocolate dots in the vast landscape, grazed contentedly as we passed by unnoticed.

In camp later that day, not yet 24 hours after the moose-caribou-wolf drama of the previous evening, we walked along an esker where spruce have taken root. We had seen tracks and scat, lots of them, sure signs of wolf activity. We saw a hole in the sand bank — the entrance to a wolf den? Our voices raised the alarm, and the wolf appeared in his doorway, not more than three metres from where we stood. He looked at each of us, scampered up the bank, atop his den, scented his territory and disappeared in silence. He acted neither threatened nor threatening. No noise, no growl, no look of anger. A minute later he reappeared on the tundra, 100 metres distant, and we watched him jog to and fro,

Alex Hall/Canoe Arctic

A crowd of caribou beside the Thelon River

all the while followed closely by a squealing short-eared owl. In due course, he stopped and picked up something dripping blood, in his mouth — we wondered if it might be the owl's mate — and headed away inland. We never saw him again, despite keeping a lookout for the next 24 hours.

As we sat down to supper that night, is it any wonder that conversation turned again to the abundance of wildlife? But it is more than that, more than the numbers. It is the natural sequence of events which is striking, the interactions between different species which we are privileged to see here. "This is more than simply viewing wildlife," I wrote in my journal that day, "this is the privilege of witnessing their life."

———————◆———————

"Canadians will surely wake up to the fact that here and here only in all of North America is to be found the thrilling and spectacular in animal life," wrote Dr. Charles Henry Douglas Clarke after his 1936-37 fieldwork in the Thelon Game Sanctuary. Clarke was the first professional biologist to examine the Thelon valley, though he is quick to acknowledge the valuable work done by his lay predecessors, including Jack Hornby and Billy Hoare.

Only the year before, Harry Snyder led an expedition by airplane which flew over the barrenlands for four days in early August, stopping to observe and photograph musk-oxen. They saw a total of 171.

In 1936, with the beginning of aerial mapping of the barrens, the government seized the opportunity to conduct a musk-ox and caribou survey. Clarke, age 27, a recent graduate from the University of Toronto with a PhD in zoology, was engaged by the National Museum and offered the assistance of an old Thelon hand, Billy Hoare, by now in his mid-40s but still a very fit traveller. That first summer, the two men did some brief flights over the sanctuary, observing and counting both caribou and musk-oxen from the air for the first time. They then landed at Crystal Island on Artillery Lake and took up temporary residence in the warden's cabin left vacant by Jack Knox four years earlier. From there they used Knox's old boat to motor up and down the western boundary of the sanctuary, gathering what biological information they could.

It was the trip out, on the barges carrying everyone south up the Slave River, that remained most vivid in Clarke's memory years later. He described it as "a carnival atmosphere. On board was everyone going outside from the entire length of the western arctic coast, the Mackenzie River, Great Bear and Great Slave Lakes. There were police, missionaries, traders, prospectors, and trappers. I had a 29 hand at cribbage, and a more auspicious company for such a happening could hardly be imagined. Everyone was vastly interested in natural history, and a memorable amount of information would have been forthcoming even if Billy Hoare had not been there. With him the trip was unique. He knew all the old timers. They were eager to talk and to ask and answer questions, and so was he. I do not consider the travel time wasted, because you could not today gather such information."

Times were changing nonetheless. The days of the old river barge crowded with northerners were fading into history. The airplane was changing everything. The next summer, Clarke and Hoare were flown north to Reliance, where they lashed their 17-foot prospector canoe to the plane, and continued on to the Hanbury's headwaters. It must have been a memorable day for Billy Hoare: the flight from Reliance to the upper Hanbury was accomplished in a few hours, a trip which had taken him four and a half months just nine years earlier. On June 21, 1937, Doug Clarke and Billy Hoare dipped their paddles into the river and began a biological investigation which took them the length of the Thelon valley, down to Baker Lake. It is a trip which stands out as a relatively modern example of the canoe used as a vehicle of scientific exploration.

Billy Hoare (left) and Doug Clarke (right), 1937

Clarke's observations are all recorded in his official report, published in 1940, which remains among the most fascinating books about the Thelon. At Warden's Grove, he estimated that the stand of spruce was at least 1,000 years old, citing one tree stump on which he counted nearly 400 rings. He saw no moose, a fact which becomes interesting in light of more recent reports of numerous sightings. They counted 21 peregrine falcon nesting sites along the river.

They saw 65 musk-oxen which, combined with the earlier aerial observations, led Clarke to suggest that the total population was approximately 300, roughly two-thirds ranging around the Hanbury-Thelon junction down to just below Hornby Point, and the other third ranging downstream of the Finnie River confluence. Most casual observers today would suggest much greater numbers, of course, with the proportional distribution exactly the reverse, that is, with the greater number downstream of Lookout Point.

"Surely if there is ever to be anything of the nature of animal husbandry in the barrens," wrote Clarke, "the domestication of the musk-ox might be one of the first steps. No animal could be more easily herded, and the value of a properly utilized carcass would be considerable. The 'wool' is unfortunately smooth and not true wool, and cannot be used by itself. However, the live animal might furnish milk, and might be comparable to the yak as a pack or saddle beast." It is ironic to consider that, although no one has tried to take commercial advantage of the musk-ox's milk or strength, the weaving and knitting of products from musk-ox wool (kiviq) has become a small but profitable enterprise elsewhere.

Clarke and Hoare intersected a herd of caribou estimated to contain between 100,000 and 200,000 animals. Clarke wrote about the caribou and their migrations at length in his official report but, years later, his lasting memory was of the "mattress of hair" that lined the riverbanks for 200 miles, suggesting immense numbers of shedding caribou had swum across the current prior to their canoe passing, in "a migration of caribou such as I fear nobody will ever see again."

Some of Clarke's ideas were ahead of his time. In decisions about wildlife management, he favoured the concerns of Native people over those of white scientists and bureaucrats. He argued against the predator control program, a scheme to kill wolves as a protective measure for the caribou. Speaking of two men who operated out of a cabin near Reliance in 1926-27, Clarke remembered that "using an immense number of strychnine baits they killed a considerable number of wolves and, naturally, a much larger number of foxes, the skins of which they were supposed to turn in with the wolf skins. They did turn in a sufficient number to allay suspicion, but sold a very large number on their own. In those days wolf poisoning and caribou management were equated."

Looking ahead to the future, a future we now live in, Clarke concluded his report with a thoughtful recommendation. "We should always be careful that in our search for new resources we do not destroy what we already have. Much of our northland will always be a wilderness. If we can keep it a true wilderness, its spiritual value will remain, but if the wild herds are lost it will not be a wilderness, but a desert."

The war years intervened, and soon it was 1950. According to John Kelsall, a young biologist with the Canadian Wildlife Service at that time, "anybody working on any mammal in the NWT had only one reference — C.H.D. Clarke's." After reading Clarke, he said, he was "hooked on the Thelon."

"I wanted a place where I could go canoeing and see caribou — I grew up in canoes in Nova Scotia," he confesses. Kelsall was intrigued by the Thelon Game Sanctuary: "Here's this huge sanctuary and we don't know what's in it. We were sort of probing around in the dark." At the time, the CWS was very open to the biologists' proposals. In 1950, it accepted Kelsall's suggestion that he go north to study the caribou of the Thelon area, and he moved north to begin plans for his investigation. His first priority, however, was a canoe trip down the Thelon.

Dr. John Kelsall, 1992

Today John Kelsall is retired and living in a sea-front home south of Vancouver. He is wheelchair bound, a result in part, he says, of so much heavy work up north, loading fuel drums into float-planes and the like. Physically restrained perhaps he is, but his spirit is still wandering the barrenlands wilderness.

Equipped with an 18-foot Prospector canoe, a 3.2HP outboard kicker (which, together with a cache of gas, was pre-positioned at the west end of Beverly Lake), the maps produced half a century earlier by J.W. Tyrrell, a rifle to be used "only for purposes of saving human life" and a huge pile of supplies, including beer, Kelsall and his partner flew in to the Hanbury-Thelon junction on July 17, 1951. They had so much gear, in fact, that the loaded canoe had only 1 1/2 inches of freeboard. So they made camp right there and stayed for a few days, eating down "the mound of grub." Using the time to advantage, they hiked across to Steel Lake, up the Clarke River, and up the Hanbury to Helen Falls. In the age old tradition of arctic travellers, there they built a cairn, which stands yet today, though the note Kelsall deposited was removed 11 years later and mailed back to the CWS in Ottawa, and the cairn has been rebuilt several times since.

Despite their efforts, they saw no musk-oxen and no caribou in the area. They did see some sign of moose. "I was pretty certain I saw moose pellets. I think I suggested that moose would be seen there sooner or later." Although there were scattered reports of moose sightings before, some of them questionable, it was not until the late seventies that those travelling in the Thelon Game Sanctuary began to see significant numbers of moose on a regular basis.

Finally, the pile of food and equipment having been reduced to a manageable amount, Kelsall and his partner, Nolan Perret, a student from British Columbia, loaded up their 18-footer. They had never paddled together. Before hiring him, Kelsall remembers checking that Perret knew how to handle a canoe, though "we never put it to the test." The time had come. Kelsall got into the stern, Perret in the bow. They pushed off and headed downriver. "I quickly asked Nolan what he thought he was doing. 'Oh,' he said, 'I'm steering the canoe.' Not only did he not have much experience in canoes, but he didn't know that you don't steer a canoe from the front! We sat there in the middle of the river and argued for quite a period of time, over how we were going to go about paddling this darn canoe. It took awhile to persuade Nolan that the thing to do was to just paddle, and let the guy in the stern do the steering. Nolan was a stubborn sort of a cuss, but he learned pretty quick."

They paddled down to Grassy Island and set up their next camp, "where we first started to see musk-oxen." In fact, they were more numerous here than at any other point on their trip. Kelsall remembers one startling encounter at this camp above all. "We were asleep in the tent and I was woken up by a bull musk-ox putting his nose against my feet through the flap of the tent. I sat up in wild alarm and gropped around for a gun, cause I didn't know what was out there. I rolled over onto my hands and knees, and looked out: there was a semi-circle of six musk-oxen standing there just staring at the tent." Between Grassy Island and Hornby Point, Kelsall saw 217 musk-oxen, all of them on the "north" side of the river.

"One time we were paddling along and there was a big bull on the bank. I thought, here's a good chance to take some snapshots, so I ran the boat ashore. I got out of the canoe and walked up a ways, lifted the camera to take a real close picture — he put his head down and came right at me! Some people say they'll never hit you [that has been fatally disproved since], but I wasn't about to take any chances. I went down the bank, grabbed the bow of that canoe and was half-way across the river by the time I got into it. The musk-ox came right down to the water's edge."

A musk-ox bull beside the Thelon River

When they stopped at the site of Hornby's demise, they found the cabin roof collapsed and the crosses marking the graves fallen over and confused. "We were a little doubtful as to which one went where," admits Kelsall. "It is conceivable that we put them on the wrong grave. We weren't certain."

The trip was, in Kelsall's words, "surely some sort of a low record for an expedition primarily interested in caribou." Over an entire month, he saw only 180, but even that gave him a better understanding of the caribou movements along and across the Thelon valley. "On the upper portion of the river we were too early ... there were abundant signs that caribou had been present in spring but not since." Below the point that has become known as "Crossing-Place-of-Deer" after a notation on Tyrrell's map, he felt he was too late to intercept a major migration.

It was at this point, just downriver from 102°W at a distinct bend to the east, near "the last impressive spruce groves worthy of mention," that Kelsall built another cairn, atop a prominent ridge on the north bank. "It was a good landmark, a place that was on the [Tyrrell] map, and it was a nice day. We caught some fish and sat down to carve a stake." The inscription reads: "J.P. Kelsall - N.G. Perret - Can. Wild. Ser. - Aug. 2 '51."

Despite the absence of exciting caribou sightings, the trip was not uneventful. "We almost came a cropper one night, just below the Finnie River," recounted Kelsall, remembering a spectacular electrical storm. "During the night the wind got even higher, and the tent started to blow away. We got up to anchor the tent and then heard the most tremendous crash. We were horrified to see the canoe being carried down the riverbank, for more than 100 yards, bouncing off rocks four feet in the air, rolling over and over — an 18-foot Prospector just flying! It was really frightening," he remembers. Eventually, they caught the canoe and tied it down — a practise Kelsall adopted as daily routine thereafter. "It wasn't till after we got back to the tent that we thought, if the wind had been blowing *toward* the river, we would've literally been up the river without a canoe."

Kelsall and Perret arrived safely in Baker Lake on August 15, and flew back to Yellowknife a few days later, surveying for caribou and musk-ox all the way. Over the whole month, they actually saw more musk-oxen than caribou, 334 in all, a surprise to everyone. Before the trip, "the feeling of barrenground trappers and bush pilots — often a good indication — was that we would be fortunate to see any." He wrote a thorough analysis of musk-ox distribution and behaviour based on that summer's observations, the conclusions of which remain essentially unchallenged today. After careful consideration, Kelsall estimated the total musk-ox population of the Game Sanctuary at 1,085, several times the estimates produced earlier by both Billy Hoare and C.H.D. Clarke. He concluded that, in a general way, the musk-oxen spend the summer feeding in the lush valley, from the Hanbury-Thelon junction all the way down to Beverly Lake. In the winter, many of them retreat into the highlands to the north.

In an official report, Kelsall wrote: "From these observations it is believed that the Thelon Game Sanctuary, which was established for the preservation of one of the last known remnants of the mainland musk-ox herds, is serving its purpose." Today, in the 1990s, with the musk-ox population *outside* the sanctuary apparently increasing, that statement continues to hold true. The sanctuary has been acting as a wildlife bank, with its growing population of musk-oxen resupplying the surrounding barrenlands.

For the rest of his northern career as a caribou biologist, Kelsall was more successful in concentrating his barrenground studies on caribou. For the next five years he attempted to determine population size and to confirm the discrete herds that been previously postulated, doing most of this work by aerial survey all over the barrenlands. In 1957/58 he organized a team of 13 men, who, travelling in three mobile camps, followed the migration of the Beverly herd back and forth across the Thelon valley for 18 months — probably the most intensive caribou study ever.

"No one [no biologist] had ever observed caribou calving," explained Kelsall. So they literally followed the caribou right up to the calving ground, north of Beverly Lake, hence the herd's name. Don Thomas was one of the team, a biologist on his first job. After following them, then watching the caribou calving during the first week of June, that herd became the focus of his work for many years to come.

Part of the Beverly caribou herd

Thomas remembers flying along transects, surveying for caribou north of Aberdeen Lake one summer, and being surprised to see a tent camp down below. "Someone came out and waved a white sheet, so we landed. But they couldn't talk. Then a woman came out of the tent with a baby in her arms and somehow indicated it was sick." Mother and child were bundled into the aircraft and flown into Baker Lake. That was Don Thomas' first contact with Inuit, but not his last; throughout the sixties he conducted caribou studies with Inuit assistants out of Baker Lake.

Kelsall did thousands of miles of flying during that period, surviving at least one crash. Frequently he visited the trappers of the upper Thelon. Sitting in his sunny west-coast living room more than 30 years later, Kelsall recalled those old fellows fondly, one tale after another bringing a smile to his face.

There was the time he dropped in on Fred Riddle, "a real nice guy," who in 1961 built the new cabin at Warden's Grove, "only he wasn't there, so we left a bottle of rum for him. His cabin was so jammed with stuff that you could hardly move." Or Gus D'Aoust, who "had the most comfortable set-up of any of them." Unlike George Magrum, up near the headwaters of the Back River, who lived in "a hovel," according to Kelsall. "He lived tough. He'd go in and shoot a caribou and put on a stew at the first of winter. Then he'd just keep adding to it all winter. It'd be a different flavour every time you went in there." The trappers provided useful and enjoyable stopping-off points for the biologists working the barrenlands. And of course the trappers, who lived a lonely existence, were always glad of the company. Since both were interested in the movement of caribou and wolves, they always had lots to talk about. "They were a tough bunch of guys," summed up Kelsall, "with a unique way of life."

The contentious issue of the day was the wolf-kill campaign. There were a lot of wolves at the time, and some biologists had suggested that the caribou population had been seriously depleted as a result. So, despite C.H.D. Clarke's arguments, now nearly 30 years old, the government decided in the early fifties to start a new "predator control program." The biologists set poisoned baits, usually caribou carcasses. "It worked," said Kelsall. "It was very efficient. I'm thoroughly convinced that we knocked the wolves down for a few years there. And for every wolf we killed, there were probably about 14 caribou that lived long enough to have calves the following spring. The wolves took a lot of caribou; that's what they lived on."

The government also paid the trappers to poison wolves. "I wasn't so happy with that part of the program," said Kelsall. "I expect those guys killed a lot of foxes in addition to the wolves. Where they were working, a fox is just as apt to come to the bait as a wolf. They weren't using big baits like we were; they were using fish and small pieces of meat. It seemed to me it was giving the guys a license to poison their fur. They took a helluva lot more fur than they would've otherwise, a lot easier."

Did it work? Yes. Was it necessary? That's doubtful. "It may be that by poisoning wolves we helped the caribou start on a rebound," reasons Kelsall. "I like to think that we did. But certainly the way they've gone — this huge increase in the numbers of caribou and musk-oxen — they would've climbed appreciably anyway. Their population seems to operate independent of how they're managed."

The Thelon's spell, cast on Dr. John Kelsall when he first read Clarke's field report, has endured all these years. "It's a romantic place," he said softly, looking out the window, searching. "When I went up north, there weren't even topographic maps of much of that country. The Thelon may be about as remote as you can get. It's unique — a wide variety of plants and animals and birds. I still wonder how John Hornby managed to starve himself to death."

With that, his voice trailed off into silence, his thoughts drifting, his eyes dreaming distant mysteries.

———————◆———————

In the late 1950s, the government of Saskatchewan decided to co-operate with John Kelsall's caribou study, and a young biologist named Ernie Kuyt (pronounced "kite") was assigned to the task. "I was not very happy about it. I didn't think I wanted to go up north!" recalls Kuyt. But north he went, flying into the Thelon Game Sanctuary for the first time in June 1957. He spent the next 18 months as part of Kelsall's team, following the caribou. It was the beginning of a love affair.

"Something must have clicked. That was my first exposure to the Barrens. We worked hard, long hours. I lost weight, thin as a rail. But on the whole it was enjoyable. It's an incredible area." When Kuyt returned to Saskatchewan, he was quick to fill in application forms for a job in Yellowknife with the Canadian Wildlife Service. In January 1960, he moved north and began work as a wolf biologist. His first task was to co-ordinate the predator control program.

"Poison is not a very appetizing way of killing," he reflects, "but it is effective. There was little concern about killing wolves in those days. Literally thousands and thousands of wolves were killed by poison. The barrenground trappers were on contract to the federal government, people like Gus D'Aoust, Fred Riddle, George Magrum — they killed wolves using poison bait."

The "best of the bunch," according to Kuyt, was Fred Riddle, the man who later built the new cabin at Warden's Grove. Kuyt remembers him as a fit, resourceful and resilient individual. Despite his job, Kuyt — a gentle giant of a man — always felt a little bad about killing wolves, but Riddle would only say "there's another sonofabitch gone."

As Kuyt put it, "Riddle did his government job better than many! He was merciless." He killed thousands of wolves. The trappers were meant to keep a record of every wolf killed, measurements and weight. "Riddle was totally unscientific," recalls Kuyt. "He'd just look at the wolf and write down some numbers, saying 'I don't need to measure it — I know wolves so well I can just tell how much it weighs.' That was Fred Riddle, a tough old bugger. There will never be another one like him."

His first summer in the new job, 1960, Ernie Kuyt and an assistant were flown out to the Thelon River, along with Kuyt's Labrador retriever, Lola, to collect data on wolf biology. Very little was known about wolves' habits at this time, even though they had been largely blamed for the decreasing numbers of caribou. During Kelsall's earlier aerial caribou studies, someone had spotted wolves around the Ursus Islands area (that name later proposed to the

Ernie Kuyt standing on the float of his plane, with the pilot behind him, 1967

Geographical Placenames Board in Ottawa by Ernie Kuyt). That summer, Kuyt and his assistant lived in tents and travelled up and down the river by canoe. Afterwards, he wrote home: "the country is absolutely beautiful," and reported sightings of musk-oxen, rough-legged hawks, ducks, geese, songbirds, and more "wonders of nature," including a remarkable fish story.

"I caught a 20-pound Lake Trout," he recorded, and "this fish's stomach contained a freshly-caught Brown Lemming *Lemmus trimucronats*. Lemming tracks were abundant on the shore of the island from which we were fishing as well as among the large boulders just above the rapids. The lemming probably slipped off one of the rocks and before it could swim to shore was swept over the rapids where the hungry fish awaited it. So not only birds and mammals prey on the abundant lemming!"

His observations that summer of geese, some of which were banded, led Kuyt to the conclusion that non-breeding Canada geese were summering on the Thelon having flown more than 2,200 air miles (3,520 km) from their winter ground in the Rio Grande valley, New Mexico. Of course, Kuyt's real purpose in being there was to study wolves, but he saw only a few.

Before leaving his Ursus Islands campsite, Kuyt, as was his habit, put some dry matches in a glass jar, sealed the lid, and left it in a hidden spot. Considering the years that Kuyt spent in the Thelon valley, one wonders how many jars of matches are hidden along the riverbanks.

One summer in the mid-1960s while Ernie Kuyt was based at Lookout Point, Don Thomas was doing his caribou work near Beverly Lake. When he finished, his Inuit assistants headed back down to Baker Lake, and he headed upriver alone to join the two men at Lookout Point. Half-way up the river, near the Ursus Islands, he swamped his small canoe. As Kuyt remembers, "Don was wearing waders, so he was very lucky to get out. He lost some of his stuff in the river, including a textbook he needed to study for a zoology exam. When he got himself to shore, soaking wet, he remembered that I'd had a camp there. So he scurried to that site and rumaged around till he found the glass jar of matches, then lit a fire and dried himself and his motor out. He arrived at Lookout Point a few days later."

After his first field season in the sanctuary, during the winter back in Yellowknife, Ernie Kuyt laid plans for a return to the Thelon in the spring, to establish a more permanent base for his studies. In May 1961, a Bristol freighter aircraft flew out to the Thelon loaded with building materials, a big freighter canoe, outboard motor, fuel and the summer's supplies, Kuyt and an assistant. They landed on the ice in a small lake across from Lookout Point. "The pilot didn't want to get close to shore, so right where the plane stopped rolling, he opened the doors and out came all our stuff. We hauled the stuff down this little creek that connects to the Thelon — a tortuous little creek, barely wide enough. There was still ice on the main river. We hauled our tents, some gear and the boat across the ice." Later, when the ice in the Thelon broke up, they were able to launch the canoe and ferry all the material over to build a cabin. That cabin became Ernie Kuyt's base for several years of fieldwork. When Kuyt finally abandoned the cabin, it stood for many more years until a grizzly bear broke in and turned everything upside down. In 1991, Kuyt visited his cabin at Lookout Point again after many years' absence and, as his final act on the Thelon, put a match to what was once his Thelon home, returning the site to nature.

During the summers from 1961 through 1965, Kuyt found only occasional wolf dens along the river, as he travelled up to Helen Falls and down to Beverly Lake. The poisoning program, apparently, had been quite effective. Over these years, wolf scat was collected and analysed to determine eating habits, 31 cubs were ear-tagged, and careful records were kept of all sightings. Some captive wolves were taken to Fort Smith, so their growth could be observed and their intake of meat measured — all part of the first study of barrenground wolves. Several of the ear-tagged cubs were later killed, having travelled some distance over the winter in pursuit of caribou, often 300 kilometres or more. Knowing the site of tagging

A *wolf beside the Thelon River*

and where the tag was recovered, confirmed for the first time biologists' belief that wolves followed the caribou migrations.

Equally interesting were the insights gained into the wolves' diet. A new-born cub depends initially on its mother's milk, but very quickly becomes interested in raw meat, which becomes their exclusive food source within about two months. In the Thelon valley, the primary prey is caribou. Musk-oxen are only infrequently attacked, much less so than smaller prey: birds, rodents and fish. Kuyt concluded that an adult wolf needs three to four pounds (1 1/2 to 2 kg) of food per day to remain healthy, and for the Thelon wolves, nearly half of that comes from caribou — in fact, almost exclusively caribou during the winter.

When a wolf attacks, it runs at a caribou and leaps for the neck or shoulder, the force of the impact knocking the caribou down to the ground. A single bite to the neck is normally enough to dispatch the caribou, and the wolf can then proceed to eat, starting with the throat area. The caribou tongue is apparently considered a delicacy among wolves. It is usually eaten right away, before the wolf moves on to open the stomach, gaining access to the organs. The fleshy parts of the caribou's hind legs are also routinely eaten before the rest of the carcass is left as carrion for other passing carnivores. Over a year, a wolf would consume about 23 caribou as a base for survival, based on Kuyt's calculated weight requirement. As it normally does not eat the whole animal, but rather leaves some for neighbouring foxes, ravens and grizzlies, the average kill is probably more, somewhere between 30 and 40 caribou in a year.

During his years of searching out wolf dens, Ernie Kuyt had several memorable encounters. He says he never, NEVER felt threatened by the wolves. In fact, when he dug down into a wolf den to get the cubs for ear-tagging, they would remain totally docile and the adults would simply stand off at a distance, watching. Timing, of course, was critical to this acceptance; Kuyt knew better than to interfere at the dens when the cubs were either too young or too mature. On one occasion, he remembers reaching down into a den and grabbing the tail of an adult wolf, with no resulting ill effects!

After 1961, the predator control program was cut back, and by 1968 it ceased altogether in the Thelon area. In 1965, Kuyt noticed a marked increase in the number of wolves sighted along the river, suggesting that already the wolf population was on the rebound. Whether it had any real effect on the caribou remains a question. Most biologists seem to agree that the caribou population undergoes some form of cyclical rise and fall, notwithstanding any human interference.

One biologist of the time, Dr. Harrison Lewis, wrote that: "wolf bounties or other measures to control wolves in those areas cannot be expected to result in substantial reduction in the number of wolves or in substantial increase in the numbers of animals on which they prey and is therefore not justified on those grounds. It is possible that it may be found desirable to expend public funds for encouragement to kill wolves for the express purpose of appeasing the public and its highly-developed and very widespread prejudices against wolves. In such scantily-populated and little-developed regions, this could be done without any danger of a serious detrimental effect on the wolf population."

Ernie Kuyt, 1992

The Thelon through the sixties was Ernie Kuyt's river. No one knew it then as he did. Today, as retirement from the Canadian Wildlife Service looms in the near future, the memory of those days is strong. He has moved on to other matters, but his Thelon file continues to grow. Wherever his attention may turn, he always keeps an eye out for what happens in the Thelon Game Sanctuary. And there is nothing he likes better, it seems, than telling Thelon stories.

In 1963 and '64, Al Oeming, owner of the Alberta Game Farm, got permission to collect six musk-ox calves each year from within the Thelon Game Sanctuary. Ernie Kuyt, since he was in there anyway, was instructed to provide a CWS presence. Kuyt remembers it well, watching the musk-oxen being herded onto a point and eventually forced into the water, in the area between the Hanbury junction and Grassy Island. A plane circling overhead would land and taxi up alongside the young musk-ox. Oeming, he says, originally made his money as a wrestling promoter, and he brought some of his "bully boys" up to the Thelon for the musk-ox catch. "They would jump out of the plane, into the water, and wrestle the musk-ox into submission, then drag it back to shore. One of the wrestlers held the musk-ox, bound up in lampwick and blindfolded, while the other man pulled a burlap sack over the beast." Six of them, bundled up this way, were loaded onto a single Otter and flown out to Yellowknife, and eventually south to his Alberta ranch. The twelve musk-oxen collected in this manner formed the basis of a breeding stock. Oeming sold musk-oxen to far-flung zoos. In 1967, one of them was sold to the London zoo; it travelled by train from Edmonton to Montreal and then across the Atlantic by ship. "Some of us were not too happy about it," recalls Kuyt.

Even though his principal focus was the wolves, Kuyt kept meticulous records all through the early sixties of other wildlife sightings, and wrote regular entries to various naturalist bulletins on his observations. His sightings included a beaver just upstream of Hornby Point, and evidence of a porcupine at Warden's Grove. He also recorded numerous raptor sightings, and was among the earlier voices drawing attention to the peregrine population decline. In the early sixties, Kuyt observed and recorded raptor nesting in the Thelon valley: at least 7 peregrine nests, 8 gyrfalcon nests, and 13 rough-legged hawk nests.

In 1966 "there was a special request to collect a clutch of eggs from one peregrine nest and kill the female," remembers Kuyt. While he was standing at the nest, the female came screaming down at him. He fired and hit. The memory obviously upset him as he continued the story. "The next year I came back and there was a single male falcon hanging around the same spot. But you're dealing with a species, not an individual. We got confirmation that there was DDT present in the tissue. That led to pressure to discontinue use of DDT in North America."

Although the hazard of DDT is now greatly reduced, the raptor population of the Thelon valley, particularly the peregrines, remains sensitive to human intrusion. A well-intentioned photographer or visitor can easily cause the adults to remain away from the nest for too long, exposing the downy chicks to extremes of either heat or cold, both of which can kill.

———————◆———————

Like most northern fieldworkers of his era, Ernie Kuyt had his share of close-calls in bush planes. He counted seven of the pilots he had flown with over the years who subsequently died in crashes. In 1961, near Gus D'Aoust's camp in the upper Thelon valley, "Wardair's Beaver hit the trees and tore a hole in one wing. It shattered the tree, but the plane kept flying and we got back to Yellowknife." He goes on, with tales of float planes hitting chunks of ice, overloaded planes running up onto riverbanks, and more, but then shrugs it all off as just another part of the job and the place. It may be, however, that surviving so many near-misses, as Kuyt did, only served to strengthen his attachment to the place.

Flying over the Thelon, perhaps for the last time, after visiting and torching his Lookout Point cabin in 1991, Ernie Kuyt looked down on the river valley he knew so well, and once called "home." Naturally, he was nostalgic.

"The work in the Thelon was always very special to me, living in such a pristine area, and being allowed to study it, was really a marvellous experience." In fact it became a part of him, or he of it. In a way, as he expressed, it was his.

"You work in the area. You *live* there. There are days when you're out in the field and a small airplane flies over and you wonder 'What the hell is that sonofabitch doing here?' You don't say it, but you feel like adding 'in my area.' I live here and I want to know what that guy is doing. I think that is a natural feeling when you love the area and feel like you own part of it. And I guess you do in some respect."

———————◆———————

One summer I set up camp along the banks of the Thelon — just where exactly is unimportant — and stayed at the same camp for a week or so. It is a completely different experience from canoeing down the river, making new camps daily. Within a few days I stumbled across several sets of discarded caribou antlers, all so bleached by the sun I surmised they had been there for years. I saw tracks: caribou, musk-ox, and wolf. I found old wolf scat just 50 metres behind our tent. I collected a good sized handful of musk-ox wool, *kiviq*, from a few branches of spruce where the animal must have scratched itself in passing. On one occasion, walking inland, my path happened upon the skeletal remains of a young caribou, perhaps a wolf kill, perhaps the victim of a broken leg in the marshy ground. One evening, walking back to camp from another exploration, I saw fresh wolf tracks right on top of my own outbound footprints in the sand. There were animals around, I knew that. Yet I had seen none. In seven days my encounters with big wildlife were limited to the vicarious.

Not that I minded. It heightened my awareness. I kept an ever watchful eye. And I continued to identify every bird I saw: 25 species in the first six days. Not bad, I felt, for an amateur. No, I did not mind at all that my list of mammal sightings was not growing; this is a wilderness with a cornucopia of moods and pleasures, challenges and highlights. No big wildlife for a few days, I thought, may help me to see everything else.

Anyway, I knew the animals were there. The signs were everywhere. And I was, after all, in the Thelon Game Sanctuary, known for its abundance of wildlife: musk-ox, caribou, moose, wolves, and grizzly bears. What I had to wonder, as day after day went by, was how many of them had seen me. In some ways, it is the amount of wildlife we do *not* see that is so impressive. The animals steal so silently, so inconspicuously, through our environs, indeed — like the wolf — right through our camp. When we do see them, they appear suddenly within our sight, having arrived within range without sound or warning. They are around, to be sure, lest we ever think we have even a corner of the sanctuary to ourselves.

11

Birchbark and Soapstone

We were camped at one of the most beautiful spots in the Thelon Oasis, about seven kilometres downstream from Grassy Island. The river sweeps south and splits around a large sandy island in mid-stream. The ridge that forms the island continues inland south of the river, climbing slowly toward an east-west oriented rocky cliff. On his map from 1900, Tyrrell labelled it "Black Mt." The dried beach lines below the base of this inland rock face show clearly that there was a time when the glacial lake flooded the Thelon valley to this depth. As the land rises above the spruce found down closer to the river, the view extends back up the river beyond the island, and on downstream where the river shallows over a sandy bottom and braided channels stand out in dark blue contrast. High over the rock face two kilometres inland a peregrine falcon beats through the air in pursuit of his prey, and dives noisily at any human intruder who might venture so far off the river. Like the peregrine, we can see for miles from this campsite, and the thought occurs naturally that perhaps the Native people before us took advantage of this fact.

As we walked up the ridge, there were signs. First a tent ring, then another, and another: stones arranged in a circle, once used to hold out the bottom skins of a tent, now embedded into the tundra. We stood still and imagined the scene. Three families, camped side by side, waiting for the caribou. Could these rings of stone be old enough to have once housed the earliest Indians to visit this territory, the Northern Plano, more than 6,000 years ago? Or their descendants, of what archaeologists call the Shield Archaic tradition, who lived here during the warm period from about 4000 B.C. until 1500 B.C.? Or were they perhaps constructed by Pre-Dorset Eskimos when they lived and hunted here as much as 3000 years ago? I had read of all these people, but my inexpert eye was not able to distinguish any diagnostic clues. Still, it was satisfying to know we were standing on the very ground where our Native predecessors had once stood. If this was our river now, it was certainly their river long before.

We walked on, past the three tent rings, up the ridge behind our beautiful campsite. Our boots crunched on the dry tundra vegetation no higher than our ankles, until we reached a small depression in the land, where the forces of nature had conspired to prevent any growth. The sand blow-out stood apart from the surrounding green tundra, catching our eye and drawing us toward it.

Lying on the surface of the sand were hundreds, if not thousands, of tiny shards of rock, mostly quartzite. Even to the rank amateur, it was obvious that Native hunters had worked here for endless hours, chipping away at their stones to fashion the blades and points needed for survival. There was no other sign of man around, but the evidence of this single patch of sand — not more than ten metres across — was compelling. It was utterly impossible to resist the urge to get down on all fours, and pick up one small piece after another. Each one held a secret. Occasionally, among the detritus of lithic manufacture, there was a greater treasure to be found: a projectile point, most often with the tip or the base broken off, sometimes a whole side missing. In any case, for one reason or another, it had been discarded: a project nearing completion, abandoned after a single mistake. The implicit patience of the hunter is astounding to the modern man.

Feeling as though we were severing our connection to a former time, an earlier civilization, we stood to go. Reluctantly we walked away from the sand, the dry tundra vegetation once again crunching softly beneath our feet. Our eyes remained cast downward, to the ground. That is where the story unfolds, on the ground: tent rings, stone fragments, bones and wood.

It was as if someone had just laid it down on top of the tundra cover. There was no immediate clue that it had been there for decades, or centuries, or possibly millenia. Our eyes caught it at the same moment, right at our feet: a perfect stone spear-tip. From its slightly concave and notched base to its sharp point, it was perfection. Along both sides, the cutting edges had been carefully formed by a rippled series of tiny chips removed along the entire length. Never before, on the tundra, have I seen such a flawless artifact. We picked it up, examined every miniscule detail. It must have been dropped unwittingly, accidentally, and its absence not noticed until later, for this spear-tip was as ready for action today as it had been on the day it was made, whenever that might have been. It could have been painstakingly manufactured in the sand blow-out we had just visited. That, we would never know.

One day, part of its mystery would be solved, I thought to myself as I carefully photographed and measured the stone point. Then we placed it back on the land where it belonged, and we left. Something in me hopes that no one else will ever stumble upon that spear-tip. Every ounce of me prays that if someone does, they will know enough to leave it there.

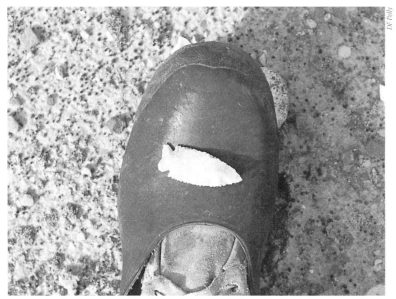

The spear-tip found in 1992 — it lies there still

Months later, I was ushered into an office on the top floor of the Canadian Museum of Civilization, with panoramic windows looking across the Ottawa River at Parliament Hill. Dr. Bryan Gordon invited me to sit. No one else has spent even a fraction of the time on archaeological fieldwork in the Thelon valley that Gordon has. He has examined and catalogued more than a thousand archaeological sites — some of them taking an entire summer to document — in the range of the Beverly caribou herd, which extends across the Thelon valley north and south.

Somewhat nervously, I handed him my best slide of *the artifact* and asked if he would be kind enough to identify it for me. With a certain professorial air, he looked at it first with the light streaming in his huge window and grunted noncommittally, then turned to a counter along one wall. There, amidst a confusion of papers, models, apparatus and what-have-you, he uncovered a viewing microscope. Magnified under intense light, the artifact sparkled again as it had on the tundra that day beside the Thelon. Its every detail was there to be seen, this time by expert eyes.

"The concave, notched base is diagnostic," he declared. To him, this was a routine identification; to me it was an exciting moment of revelation. "It's from the late Taltheilei period." Side-notching, such as "our" point had, according to Gordon, first occurred along the Thelon about 800 A.D. The spear-tip or arrowhead we found may date back a thousand years. It was made by the Indians who are the ancestors of today's Dene.

In the late 1960s, Bryan Gordon was a graduate student at the University of Calgary. Someone on Al Oeming's musk-ox expedition to the Thelon valley had picked up some quartzite stone tools, and brought them into the university. Bryan Gordon was asked to look at them, "rather crude biface knives, nothing you could really say much about," he remembered. But the event raised questions in the archaeological minds at the university; what people might have made these knives? As Gordon put it back then, "I really don't know, but the only way to find out is to go up there." It was a new frontier for archaeologists. Plans were laid to begin archaeological fieldwork in the Thelon valley.

"One of the problems of going into the Thelon was simple logistics," recalled Gordon, 25 years later, sitting in his palatial office overlooking the Ottawa River. "By the time you got a single Otter [float plane] loaded with enough gas to get in and back [to Yellowknife], you can't take much of a load. So I had to overcome this problem."

Gordon knew he would need to be in there for at least a couple of summers, with a crew, field equipment, boats, fuel drums, medical supplies, etc. — far too much for a single Otter float plane. So he asked the Department of National Defence for help, and they offered a Hercules transport plane. Anticipating his gear requirements for three years of summer work in the Thelon, he loaded everything on a huge steel pallet. The military probably called it a training flight, but in late May of 1970 a Hercules came down low to the ground over the Thelon valley, and right in front of Warden's Grove the crew pushed the pallet out the plane's back door. The pallet is still there today, a porch of sorts in front of the cabin Fred Riddle built in 1961. The cabin became Bryan Gordon's crew's headquarters, the pallet became the kitchen. There are also two red boxes marked "Upper Thelon Archaeology Project, University of Calgary," which originally contained some of Gordon's equipment, that still sit on the ground beside the cabin.

About a week after the Hercules drop, Gordon and his crew flew in. "We got in there a day after the ice went out. There were big floes along the bank. We tied the float-plane up against the ice floes." Within days, their initial investigations revealed an archaeological treasure trove. "As soon as we started looking around, after settling into our camp at Warden's Grove, we crossed the river and started finding sites all over. Then it became a matter of picking and choosing which ones we wanted to surface collect and which ones we wanted to dig." They excavated the site that became officially known as KjNb-6, "a tiny site" that eventually produced 2,667 artifacts, on the point right across from Warden's Grove.

"We went down to Hornby's Point by boat. It took us about four days, down and back, surveying along the river on both sides." In all they found 52 sites between the Hanbury-Thelon junction and Hornby Point. Travelling by foot, by canoe, and for a few days in mid-summer by air when the re-supply plane came in, they surveyed much of the surrounding country. As Bryan Gordon put it, "the area around Warden's Grove, I think we know pretty thoroughly."

Gordon went on to explain that the hunters, whose artifacts he was finding, usually positioned themselves on the "receiving" side of the river, to await the caribou as they emerged from swimming across. Around Warden's Grove, most of the archaeological evidence was, correspondingly, on the south side of the river, suggesting that in times past, as today, the caribou approached from the northeast, heading generally south. Today, sometime about July 18-21 most summers, there is still a massive southbound movement of caribou across the river at this point.

After a little more than a month in the field, Bryan Gordon and his crew packed up to leave but, realizing they had really only begun to scratch the surface, he knew he would be back. The next year, 1971, Gordon was determined to manage a longer field season. One of the people he recruited to his crew was Bob Janes, a new graduate student in archaeology at the University of Calgary, who had been on only one dig before, on an island in Lake Michigan. Janes remembers his excitement: "we were constantly enthralled by the place." Before heading north, he had convinced his new boss that his girlfriend from the United States, who could draw after all, should come along too. So in the spring of 1971, Bob Janes and Priscilla Bickle, who had just graduated from college in Colorado where she studied Art, were driving north up the gravel highway toward Yellowknife, passing through forest fires and dealing with blown-out tires, headed for adventures unknown in the Thelon Game Sanctuary. So far as they can remember, they were volunteer labour, there for the experience. "This was our introduction to the North — we felt it was a privilege to be there." As it turned out, their lives remained intertwined with the North for 15 years after that.

It is not surprising that that summer remains fixed in their minds. "We worked hard," they remember, 12 hours a day, six days a week. Often, on Saturday evening, the young couple would pack a knapsack and hike up into the hills to be alone for their 24-hour day off. There were wolves and musk-oxen around and a herd of about 10,000 caribou passed right by their tents at Warden's Grove — "it was a real eye-opener." Apart from sketching the sites and the artifacts, Priscilla made herself useful around Bryan Gordon's camp: or as she put it, "I cooked his meals and took care of his kid!" Gordon and his wife Midge had their two-year-old daughter Charlotte with them, as did another couple, so it was quite a family scene, with diapers hung to dry on the line, the *Joy of Cooking* on the cabin shelf, and strains of Neil Young and Judy Collins wafting out of the tape player. Nevertheless, there was lots of archaeology accomplished.

The crew excavated several more sites in the area, and patterns began to emerge in Gordon's analysis. By the end of that summer, they had collected 5,906 artifacts from 18 of their sites. "Since it was a new area," admitted Gordon, "there were tools that I couldn't tell what culture they were. Pre-Dorset [Eskimo] was easy, cause it's mostly chert. So was some of the Taltheilei and Chipewyan pre-historic material. But when you got to the lower levels in the digs, there was material there that I wasn't sure of. It turned out to be Shield Archaic [the ancestors of those early Indians who eventually migrated south as far as Arizona and New Mexico], which was also found later way downstream. It's earlier than pre-Dorset. There were surface finds of even earlier material, dated about 6,000 BC."

The Pre-Dorset Eskimo material (or Arctic Small Tool Tradition) was concentrated at the sites near Warden's Grove. In that area alone, Gordon found more than a thousand artifacts made by these people about 3,000 years ago, give or take a couple of hundred years. But there has been evidence of their presence all the way down the river.

In fact, Gordon was able to conclude from his finds that the obvious caribou crossings, like the one at Warden's Grove, had been used for thousands of years by successive groups of hunters. People lived in camps right along the present day riverbank 8,000 years ago. That is not long after the last ice age; the upper Thelon was still under the glacier 9,000 years ago. "The drainage process was probably fast and probably stabilized very quickly. Once the ice barriers had broken downstream, the river was very similar to what it is today," explained Gordon.

At KjNb-6, for example, across from Warden's Grove, Gordon's team dug down through and recorded at least five distinct stratified cultural levels. In effect, as they excavated deeper, they went back in time, the artifacts buried in layer upon layer of accumulated sand, soil, and old humus.

At most of the sites his team examined, they found artifacts from a mixture of different time periods and various cultural groups. "That is the rule, rather than the exception," says Gordon. "Because it's a caribou water-crossing, and because hunters in the past were familiar with how the caribou migrated, they're all [the different cultures, through time] going to be at that same crossing." It is the same all the way down the river to Beverly

Lake. All the hunting cultures through history who used the Thelon valley, claims Gordon, would have followed the caribou out toward the calving ground north of Beverly Lake.

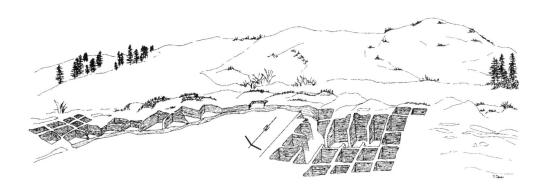

The KjNb-6 site across the river from Warden's Grove   *Priscilla Janes*

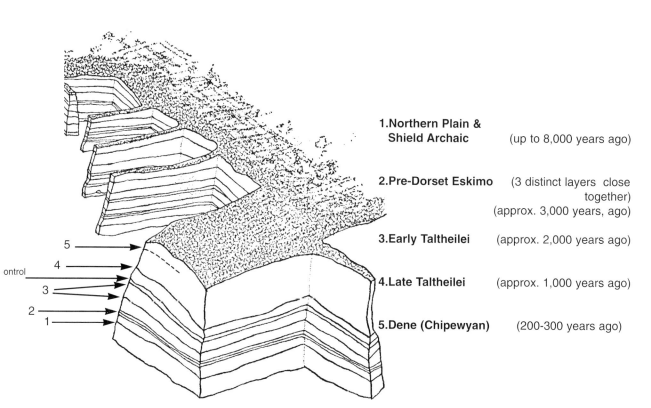

1.**Northern Plain &
Shield Archaic**   (up to 8,000 years ago)

2.**Pre-Dorset Eskimo**   (3 distinct layers close
together)
(approx. 3,000 years, ago)

3.**Early Taltheilei**   (approx. 2,000 years ago)

4.**Late Taltheilei**   (approx. 1,000 years ago)

5.**Dene (Chipewyan)**   (200-300 years ago)

The layers of occupation inside the excavated trench of KjNb-6   *Priscilla Janes*

"I don't think everybody would go to the calving grounds. I think some would wait along the river and ambush the caribou as they returned. I think it was a social division, based on agreement among the hunters as a group, to maximize their yield. But there are sites all up and down the river, right down to Aberdeen." The caribou, it is clear, are central to the archaeology of the Thelon valley.

"I think the herd [on its return from the calving ground] probably followed the river upstream across from Warden's Grove. The main body of animals went south, down to around Rennie and Damant Lake, which is actually the old homeland of the Ethen-eldili."

Gordon's crew worked late that summer, 1971, anxious to compile as much data as possible. Winter threatened to arrive early; ice began to form on the ponds. Bryan Gordon got concerned about their pick-up plane getting in; he knew the history of Warden's Grove, and Billy Hoare, and John Hornby. But his anxiety was no match for Priscilla's; she and Bob Janes had plans to drive back to Minnesota to get married.

As Bryan Gordon spoke of the Caribou-Eaters, I looked once again at the photograph in my hands of the arrowhead found beside the Thelon River. It was made and dropped there by their immediate ancestors, the very people who established the cycle of life that had endured for the Ethen-eldili since before the time of Christ. To them, the river was *The-lew-dezeth*, a focal point of their lives.

In April or May, when the warmth of the spring sun could be felt once again, the eldest of the active hunters in the Ethen-eldili camp at the forest edge decided that the time had come. The meat was growing scarce by then, and people looked forward to fresh caribou. Activity heightened, as the women packed up the camp and the men prepared their hunting weapons. Even the long poles used to erect the skin tipis must be taken, for they would be camping soon in the land without trees. In a matter of days the hunting group — men, women, and children — was on the move. Like the caribou, the Ethen-eldili took advantage of the still-frozen lakes and rivers to facilitate their northward march. Everyone who could, walked, using snowshoes in the soft snow of the taiga. An infant was carried by its mother, under her clothing against the naked skin. If a pregnant woman gave birth along the way, it would be only a matter of hours before she was back on her feet. In addition, women pulled the toboggans and carried loads on their backs.

Apart from making the decisions about travel, men were the providers, pure and simple. They hunted and fished. Enough caribou were taken from the spring aggregations to last the families through the summer; the women dried and pounded the meat as the group moved slowly northward. The destination of this annual shift was pre-ordained: while some would follow the great herd right onto the calving ground, others would wait where the caribou could be hunted in great numbers when the herd came south again later in the summer.

Travelling with a group of hunters was the key to survival. The hunting tactic favoured for more than two thousand years by the people of the Taltheilei tradition required a communal effort. Their principal weapon was a lance or spear. Bows and arrows were secondary, and used mainly for smaller game like ptarmigan.

In the spring, great herds of caribou were starting their northern trek toward the open barrenlands, making it relatively easy to kill large numbers. Most often, two long lines of cut trees or brush served as converging fences to direct the prey into a pound or corral. Sometimes natural declivities of rock could be used in the same manner. Once the caribou were entrapped, the Indians could despatch them simply by spear or, failing that, jump on the animals' backs and manually strangle them.

As the rivers and lakes melted in June, the open water created a new barrier to travel. Unlike their Cree neighbours to the south, the Ethen-eldili and their ancestors did not build large birchbark canoes for river travel. They walked overland, and used either small canoes or rafts to cross open water that barred their way. The vessels were light and small so they could be carried, probably made with caribou skins over a wooden frame about four metres long.

By early summer, several hunting groups gathered together at an established caribou ambush, most likely where the herd must ford a river. To this day, the land bears the imprint of the many millions of caribou who have passed through such places over thousands of years. As many as ten or twelve tents, housing more than a hundred people, formed a barrenlands summer camp. Several such camps were established, each at a different water-crossing. And then the waiting began.

When the caribou arrived, huge herds of many tens of thousands, they moved along the riverbank or lakeshore until they found a suitably narrow crossing place. Narrows, islands and peninsulas all served to attract them. The hunters lay in wait, usually on the far bank, sometimes with a pound set up to trap the caribou. If there was an island in mid-stream, that too made a good site for ambush. While the hunters lurked on one bank, the animals accumulated on the other, as the leading adults hesitated to enter the water. The hunters watched in silence, preparing their weapons. Eventually the pressure of so many caribou catching up from behind forced the leaders into the water, and then a steady stream of animals followed.

Sometimes, particularly at wider, deeper crossings where the caribou were obliged to swim some distance, the Indians would take to their tiny canoes, two men to a boat, one to manage the paddle, the other to wield the spear. It was a tricky, dangerous way to hunt, for the canoes were unstable, the caribou strong swimmers, and the water icy cold. More typically, the hunters remained ashore, concealed behind bushes, rocks, and natural landforms, perhaps at several points along the caribou's path. In a successful hunt, the men took enough animals to supply all the families in their camp with meat, and probably had extra to offer other camps whose water-crossing ambushes had not been so productive.

Once the caribou were slain and skinned, the men's job was done. It was women's work to dress the meat and prepare the hides to be sewn into winter clothing. Certain superstitious traditions attended their task. A woman cutting up a caribou carcass must be careful where she places her knife; should it mistakenly get caught under her clothing, as she squats on the ground beside the meat, more caribou will not migrate through the district that year. Before she begins to cut up the meat, a woman first pierces the animal's eyeballs, so that the dead caribou's spirit will not watch the butchering and thus be able to warn the rest of the herd what fate awaits.

The most important hunt took place in late August and September, by which time the caribou had reached the vast area surrounding the headwaters of the Thelon. The weather was getting cooler again as autumn advanced. The caribou were fatter and their coats were in prime condition for winter. To the Ethen-eldili, this meant good meat and quality skins for clothing. Success at the fall hunt was the key to surviving the long winter ahead, even as the hunting groups dispersed once again to their separate winter camps at the forest-edge.

Life hung in a delicate balance between man and caribou. The cycle continued thus for hundreds of years, the Ethen-eldili driven by the urge to survive. Without the animals, the Caribou-Eaters would never have known the *The-lew-dezeth*.

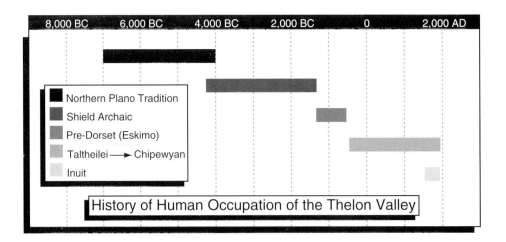

| 8,000 BC | 6,000 BC | 4,000 BC | 2,000 BC | 0 | 2,000 AD |

Northern Plano Tradition
Shield Archaic
Pre-Dorset (Eskimo)
Taltheilei ⟶ Chipewyan
Inuit

History of Human Occupation of the Thelon Valley

"In the prehistoric period [before, say, the 18th century] the Thelon River above Beverly Lake was Chipewyan territory," says Bryan Gordon. "I think they ceased using much of the river because of decreasing population and being pulled into the fur-trade in the forest to the south. Then the Inuit went upstream somewhat." Bryan Gordon believes that Inuit moved south into the Thelon valley, from farther north near the arctic coast, sometime in the 1700s. If that is the case, they almost certainly would have encountered the Chipewyan hunters following the caribou each spring onto the calving ground north of Beverly Lake. At some point, it seems highly likely that there was regular contact between the two cultures, Inuit and Chipewyan, much of the time friendly and involving some co-operation and trade, most likely centred around Beverly Lake, near the calving ground. Chipewyan obtained the soapstone for pipe bowls and, later, sled dogs, from their Inuit neighbours, who in return received birchbark.

In fact, there is at least one historical record of such interaction between Inuit and Chipewyan. The explorer Thomas Simpson writes of a meeting "of the most amicable character, and they spent a great part of the summer together" in 1836 at the confluence of the Dubawnt with the Thelon, on the south shore of Beverly Lake.

Certainly, in the sites discovered and examined by Bryan Gordon and his crew along the stretch of river above Beverly Lake, there was "some give and take of cultural boundaries between Chipewyan and Inuit." At some locations between Lookout Point and Beverly Lake, there is evidence of both Inuit and Chipewyan presence in the same site.

Over the years following the summer of 1971, Bryan Gordon's future surveys searched north and south of the Thelon, eventually covering most of the range of the Beverly herd. In total he documented 1,004 archaeological sites and hundreds of thousands of artifacts. Reflecting back over his own 12 years in the Thelon region, combined with the work of others, Gordon suggests the Thelon is "probably the most surveyed river in the Northwest Territories."

Eric and Pamela Morse, leaders of the first modern-day recreational canoe trip on the Hanbury-Thelon River, 1962

12

The canoeists

By the summer of 1962, his third summer of living and working the length of the Thelon valley's stretch through the game sanctuary, Ernie Kuyt was beginning to feel, as he put it, that "I live here and I want to know what that guy is doing ... in my area." So perhaps it is not surprising that he had himself positioned at the foot of Helen Falls on the Hanbury River, leisurely fishing, to "welcome" Eric Morse and his party of canoeists when they arrived in the sanctuary.

Eric Morse and his fellow "voyageurs," as they became known, had pushed recreational canoe tripping in Canada to new frontiers. For several years, they had been following old fur trade routes into and across the northwest. An historian by training, Morse's bookshelves were lined with the accounts of early northern explorers. Having read Hanbury and Tyrrell, and knowing the legend of John Hornby, Morse dreamed of paddling across the Barrens from the Mackenzie watershed to Hudson Bay. His only glimpse of the barrens had been from an airplane window, while flying north of Yellowknife in the course of another summer's canoe trip. Being the adventurer he was, Morse was inextricably drawn to it. Plans inevitably took form in his head for a descent of the Thelon River, a route which would traverse the Barrens.

"It had not been easy to recruit our team for this journey. My earlier companions," he wrote later, referring to the voyageurs, "were not attracted to the Barrens." In the end, he assembled a party of four: his wife Pamela Morse, plus Arch Jones, and as a last minute replacement, Bill Nicholls, who had never been in a canoe.

Eric read the diaries of Edgar Christian and Billy Hoare, and realized the immensity of his undertaking. If he did not want to endure the hardships they had, he knew that every

Eric and Pamela Morse on the upper Hanbury, 1962, in a cedar-canvas canoe

detail would require careful planning. Pamela took responsibility for organizing the food which, given the fates of their predecessors on the Thelon, seemed a worrisome task. "I'd never done provisioning for an arctic trip before," she reminisced years later. "I wondered if I had my sums right. I was scared I wouldn't be able to feed people enough." She too had read Edgar Christian's diary.

On July 14, 1962, they flew to Sifton Lake, near the headwaters of the Hanbury River. Despite meticulous planning, it was very much an adventure into the unknown. Their maps for the trip, the best available at the time, were eight miles to the inch, marked "provisional." Eric Morse had prepared a careful navigation plan, calculating their intended progress by stages all the way down the Hanbury and Thelon to Baker Lake. A few days later, at the portage around Helen Falls, Morse found the cairn built in 1951 by the biologist John Kelsall. He wrote a short, understated note, which has survived the years. It signals the dawning of recreational canoeing in the Thelon Game Sanctuary.

> *Pamela & Eric Morse*
> *Bill Nicholls*
> *Arch Jones*
> *July 21ˢᵗ 1962*
> *en route*
> *Baker Lake*
> *by canoe.*

Morse carried Tyrrell's account and read aloud from it during moments of leisure. It was not a leisurely trip, however, as Morse described it. "Up at 5 am, we breakfasted well, and could be off by 7 o'clock. Sustained by glucose tablets at our *pipes* and portages, we would lunch at about noon, making just an hour's stop. At 'teatime' the snack was supplemented by chocolate, dried fruit, or cheese. There was a delightful freedom from the accustomed pressure of having to make camp before dark, though commonsense directed an early enough camp to get a good eight-hour sleep." They travelled quickly. The 180 kilometre stretch from the Hanbury-Thelon junction to Lookout Point, for example, they covered in three days.

Eric Morse

The Morse trip, during a break along the stretch of the Thelon below Lookout Point. Pamela is standing by the canoes, Arch Jones and Bill Nicholls are walking in the distance

They saw no one else in the sanctuary that summer, except Ernie Kuyt at Lookout Point, who had returned to his base by motor-boat. Over dinner at his cabin, a curious Kuyt asked the Morses what a canoe trip like theirs cost. About $1,200 each, estimated Morse, including travel to the North, air charter, canoe rental and food. A smile spread slowly over Kuyt's face. "And to think they *pay* me to be here!" he said.

Two days later, 110 kilometres farther downstream, they were back out in the Barrens, ready to cross Beverly Lake, when the weather stopped them. "Unable to proceed because of violent winds," wrote Morse in his diary. The next day he continued: "Still pinned down. Rain and strong wind all day... Wind dropped by 6. At 8 pm set off and paddled around N. shore of Beverly L. Still raining and blowing from NW. Stopped at 12:30 am, 16 miles down L. Camped on beach & had four hours sleep." They were up again at 6 am, and skipped breakfast in order to make a quick start.

Not unlike many canoe-trippers since, Morse and his party enjoyed the wildlife and the tranquility of the sanctuary, welcomed the sight of the treeless barrenlands as the Thelon leaves the Oasis, and then encountered the formidable, windswept lakes. Like many since, they were pinned down and severely delayed by the winds on Aberdeen Lake — in their case, worse than most. Morse's diary describes, with mounting frustration, a 9-day blow of gale force winds. Three days before they were due in Baker Lake, Eric Morse sent a note out (in a passing motorboat[*] — the only one they saw) to the RCMP in Baker Lake:

> Pinned down by strong winds near east base of big peninsula on
> Aberdeen L. Cannot make rendezvous at foot of Schultz L. Prepared
> to abandon our canoes unless wind allows us to proceed.

Despite everything, they made it, with a couple of marathon paddles on the final days, arriving in Baker Lake on August 6, in time to catch their scheduled flight south.[§]

This stalwart group — three men and a woman — was the first to undertake a recreational trip of this nature. The example they set and the lessons they learned have served hundreds of others who have followed in their wake. Eric Morse turned 58 the year he led the first recreational canoe trip down the Thelon. In subsequent years, he paddled several other northern rivers, and unwittingly but deservedly gained recognition as a pioneer of wilderness canoeing in Canada. He will be remembered for a long time.

In the cairn at Helen Falls, where Morse's note is the oldest survivor, many of his successors have left their own records, some poetic, some strictly factual. By the time Pamela and Eric Morse passed this way again in 1973, there were 20 notes added to the collection. Over the years since there have been many more, including former Prime Minister John Turner and his family in 1978; Billy Hoare's daughter Sheila Hoare Thomson in 1978; the first all-women trip

---

[*] *This boat contained Andrew Macpherson, a biologist with the Canadian Wildlife Service, his wife Elizabeth, and their Inuit guide Seeteenak. From 1959 to 1963, Macpherson worked generally in this area, out of Baker Lake, studying foxes and lemmings. He spent a lot of time at Aberdeen Lake, where he had a cabin, just north of the river's entrance. Something of that cabin still remains.*

[§] *In retrospect, their schedule of 23 days from Sifton Lake to Baker Lake seems too short. Anyone planning such a trip would be well advised to allow significantly more time.*

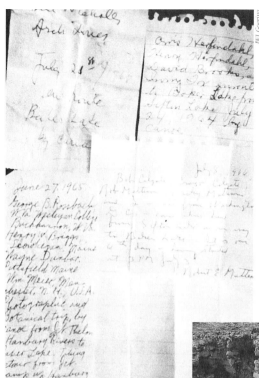

JWL Goering

Notes left in the cairn from 1962, '64, '65 & '66

DF Pelly

The cairn at Helen Falls

in 1979; former Prime Minister Pierre Trudeau in 1979; Alex Hall on no less than ten occasions; John Hornby's great-nephew Tom Hornby Hill in 1984; The Duke and Duchess of York (a.k.a. Andrew and Fergie) in 1987; and trippers from Canada, the U.S.A., Japan, Sweden, Germany, France and Britain. The lure of the Thelon has evidently spread far and wide.[*]

[*] *A book containing facsimiles and typescripts of the notes accumulated in the Helen Falls cairn from 1962 to 1992 is planned for publication by Betelgeuse Books, Toronto in 1996.*

Some of the early recreational trippers on the Thelon have left behind accounts, in one form or another, some published and some not, of their journeys. They offer varied insights into the experiences of these paddlers. Why do we go there? I believe what we seek, consciously or not, is a deluge of sensations: of pleasure and pain, of tedium and excitement, of humility and triumph, of terror and tranquility. It is an adventure of the spirit as much as of the body.

Orris Herfindahl (with Henry Herfindahl, 13, David Brooks and Irving Fox, all from Washington, DC) for four weeks from Sifton Lake to Baker Lake, 1964.

"The rules for survival are very simple: Never get committed in a rapid unless you know what is ahead and know that you can recover boat, gear, and yourself if you dump. On the Hanbury River there are numerous places where violation of this rule will produce a quick death. These are the places where one portages...

"Although every bend in the river brought a new vista, the daily routine was much the same over the whole trip. When we rose at about 6 am, the sun had already been up for hours, since we were just a few degrees below the Arctic Circle. We would light the fire, using driftwood or Arctic willow, and get the coffee going...

"We would start paddling about one-and-a-half to two hours after arising. In mid-morning we would stop for a short rest and get out of the canoes to walk around. This was especially welcome since we kneel while paddling ...

"All this no doubt sounds like a great deal of hard work, perhaps rather boring. Hard work it was, but never boring. It is a memorable experience to be in the midst of the Barrens several hundred miles from civilization and to know that your return depends on your own effort..."

George Rossbach (with Henry Briggs, Wayne Dunbar, William Meier, all from the eastern U.S.) for five weeks from the Hanbury-Thelon junction to Baker Lake, 1965.

"We ascended the turbulent Hanbury on a scenic overnight detour for about ten miles to 60-foot Helen Falls. I found here the cairn and notes of the two recent parties who had canoed these rivers, led by Eric Morse in 1962, and by Irving Fox in 1964. We sat behind a flimsy screen of white spruce and twice watched huge grizzlies poke along the shore, swim the swift, cold river, and sit on the opposite bank. Both eventually sniffed us, and ran off over the barrens at an amazing speed—in the *other* direction. We heard the whistled songs of Harris's sparrow, which nests only at treeline, and songs of tree sparrows, white-crowned sparrows, grey-cheeked thrushes, at least one kind of warbler, and even robins...

"White and black spruce form scattering lines or clumps along the Thelon almost as far as Beverly Lake. Stumps at Warden's Grove have a hundred and more rings. Here stand three log cabins, two old and crumbling, one very new. Leaning against an old one was a toboggan. On it was printed: W.H.B. Hoare, a reminder of earlier men associated with the Thelon Game Sanctuary through which we were passing...

"One of the most delightful groves is one near which we camped northeast of Hornby Point. The big spruce grow along a cascade brook in a ravine. The nearby open barrens, as usual in early July, were gaudy with the bright purplish pink flowers of the dwarf Rhododendron called Lapland rosebay and the low, white clusters of the small-leaved arctic Labrador tea, but in and bordering the local woods I found twinflower, a columbine, and the only patch of red raspberry and white-flowered currant that I saw on the trip east of Great Slave Lake.[*] It was here we found the winter droppings of a moose, and just upriver the conspicuous gnawings of porcupines. Moose have been reported by Eskimos east to Beverly Lake, but it is said no white man has seen one on the Thelon...

"Eight miles northwest of Aberdeen Lake we camped by some hunting Eskimos. Eskimos here still live on caribou. They dry strips of meat and split long bones for marrow, often eating both raw, along with bannock and tea. They are generally very pleasant people, and though rather shy, not diffident. Few speak any English. Most are literate in their own Inuit [Inuktitut], using a missionary's syllabics. These people often wear caribou skin boots, mittens, and parkas. Eskimos also wear Hudson's Bay Company woollens and rubber boots. Many of the men smoke pipes, most purchased at the Hudson's Bay store at Baker Lake, but some home-made with soapstone bowls...

"Deterrents to progress were wind, usually north, and dangerous waves. Waves often kept us ashore, as did endless pack-ice on Aberdeen Lake from July 15 to 26. We waited for a total of over two weeks for wind to abate, or to rise and blow away the ice. Hold-ups afforded me time to explore afoot, collect and dry plants, and write diary. I was never idle for long."

---

* Such finds are a hallmark of the Thelon Oasis. There is a similar ravine, nearly 20 km upstream from Hornby Point, where a small stream cascades down into the Thelon from the south, where I have found similar growth: raspberry, currant, and columbine, all considerably north of their "official" range.

Ian MacLaren, 16 (with Jack Goering and Pete Ferguson as leaders, plus Ken Biggs, Bill Orr, Danny Sawyer, Robert Sculthorpe and Dave Thompson, all 16-year-old trippers from Onondaga Camp in Minden, Ontario) for four weeks from Sifton Lake to Baker Lake, 1967.

"This was the premier celebration of Canada's centennial for Onondaga Camp. What better place than the Thelon's wilderness for Canadians to acknowledge their gratitude for being born in this great land?

"Jack Goering was a good friend of Eric and Pamela Morse. Pamela prepared the food list for the trip and Jack arranged the other logistical details, with pointers from Eric...

"Not only did we have to come to terms with the death of Edgar Christian, who was just slightly older than us when he died with Hornby and Adlard, but also we began to learn about life far beyond civilization. Sure, we were young and rambunctious and, like most our age, spent too much of our time fantasizing over the first restaurant meal once we got out, but we were learning to live on a new set of terms, ones that startled us for their beauty, ferocity, and their indomitable force. No doubt, I wasn't the first to meet God on his natural terms on the Thelon.

"With Jack Goering's skills as a teacher of natural science to encourage us, we gradually metamorphosed from anthropocentric river-baggers counting mileage on our maps, into students in a wilderness laboratory. We witnessed a huge portion of the Beverly caribou herd — paddling along, our noses told us we were downwind of something formidable, but it seemed like hours before we beached our canoes, climbed up a rise, and at last saw them, covering the tundra right to the horizon. We were fascinated near the Ursus Islands to see a herd of muskoxen circle in their customary defensive posture — calves in the middle — and then stampede down to the shore to frighten off the intruders. Similarly memorable were the Dickson Canyon and the virtually traditional three days spent windbound on one of the lakes. Like nearly everyone before or since, except for the haunting experience at Hornby's cabin, we felt we were the first people ever to venture down that river."

Keith Acheson, (with Mike Thompson, Walter Gunn, Ash Winter, Jim Boone, Bob Miller, Bill Spragge, & Dave Storey, all of southern Ontario) 24 days from Sifton Lake to Baker Lake, 1969.

"Eric Morse, the dean of Canadian canoeists who has paddled almost every river route in Canada, agreed to take us on a shakedown trip. We rented canoes at an outfitter's in Algonquin Park who filled us with horror stories concerning the Petawawa. However, Eric Morse did a superb job of teaching us how to 'read' white water and manoeuvre in the rapids...

"As we circled to land on Sifton we saw what we did not expect nor want to see —
ice. The next day we paddled along the edges where openings existed and dragged or
'scootered' our canoes over the ice where they did not. The aluminum canoes took a terrible
beating on the ice but held together admirably...

"The last half of the Hanbury River was a crazy joy ride. I swear the river is tilted. As
our canoes sped down we took a series of small rapids with our ears cocked for the roar of
the three large waterfalls and one canyon that had to be portaged. If we didn't take out in
time there would be little chance of surviving...

"The Thelon is a much bigger river which has some languid as well as turbulent
stretches. It stands out in my memory for two reasons: the ruins of John Hornby's cabin and
the variety of wildlife. The ruins of the cabin and the three shallow graves with their crude
crosses made a lasting impression on all of us. Many of the stumps around the cabin bore
the marks of being cut by someone who had little experience with an axe — probably
Christian. With our freeze-dried food, our aluminum canoes, light weight Arctic sleeping
bags and other modern gear we felt uneasy in the presence of Hornby's spirit. Until then we
had almost persuaded ourselves that we were really roughing it...

"The Thelon abounds with birds and animals. In this northern masquerade the
musk-ox wins the door prize for best costume. When the wind was in our favour, we were
able to get very close to these hairy beasts. Although it would be unwise to rub noses with a
lone musk-ox bull, the only animal that presents a potential danger to man in the Barren
Ground is the grizzly bear. At almost every campsite we saw bear tracks. Our gear included
a large revolver in case we ever encountered a bear who found us attractive. However, it
would have taken at least five minutes to dig the gun out in an emergency and I'm sure a
grizzly can do a lot of eating in five minutes. The gun was fired only once — to announce the
unpacking of some chocolate covered grasshoppers that were to accompany our overproof
rum version of a cocktail...

"A horde of smiling Eskimo children welcomed us to Baker Lake. For twenty-four
days we had not used money, were unaware of world crises, and had gazed at the moon and
wondered whether man had been successful in his brazen attempt to capture her. Now we
were buying souvenirs, asking how the Expos were doing and listening to accounts of the
American achievement..."

Geills Turner (with John N. Turner, Elizabeth Turner, 14, Michael Turner, 12, David Turner, 10, from Toronto plus Bob Engle, Bill Wightman, & Steve McGinnes) 13 days from Sifton Lake to the Thelon junction, 1978.

"As the plane door opened we were suddenly surrounded by the most incredible hordes of giant mosquitoes and tiny black flies. They are merciless and one understands how people have been driven crazy by them. Everyone put on what was available. Three head nets and some cheese cloth. What a sight we all made. Dinner preparations started with a sense of purpose. After things were underway, I went to the tent to write, with the cooking noises around us...

"August 8 ... We set off at 11:30 — not an impressive start. It took us until 2 pm to find the river narrows with much map consultation and a visit to a height of land.

"August 9 ... 7 am. Today I had my first bath and hair wash. The water was bloody cold and it was no particular consolation to hear that it is warmer than Slave [Great Slave Lake]. I did the usual wetting, soaping, wetting and came out rather quickly into the waiting arms of JNT and the black flies...

"On we went across Lac du Bois — a pretty lake with many rocks which seemed to march out to the middle of the lake and which made the paddling tricky at times. We went through some fast water which everyone loved...

"The bugs were never worse and there wasn't a breath of wind. The kids had begun to go squirrely with the bugs and there was talk of going home.

"August 10 ... As we pushed off into Hanbury Lake it was like the beginning of a new adventure. Hanbury Lake is smallish and round in shape. We set off down the south shore. There was a nice breeze blowing coming from the north...

"The river widened out and narrowed in alternatively each time with the current speeding up, which meant a fun, fastish run. After lunch we set off. We had to retrace our steps a bit so as to go around an island. We had to drag the canoes through. JNT is always the first to get in there and get wet...

"We approached Macdonald Falls. As we heard the sound of rushing water we pulled into the left shore to inspect. We picked our lunch spot on some flat rocks overlooking the first falls. Lots of photos, etc. As it was hot and there was a sandy bottom above the falls, we all had a swim/bath. Steve and Bill went swimming over the rocks and we all did one - all nude 'cept me who wore the bathing suit. We ate standing up looking into the wind to fight the bugs...

"August 15 ... Up early (never know the time) and wrote in journal. Warm, sunny day, which the bugs would be loving. JNT first up as usual — about 7:30. Our big day for the Dickson Canyon had arrived...

"I set off, once we hit high ground, to see the canyon. It seemed a shame to miss it. I followed it upstream. Each turn was more incredible than the last. Thundering water through the narrow, very high gorge — twisting and turning with such force through the beautiful pink, red rock. At one point, a jut of land went right out to the middle of the canyon. I went to the tip and could see both ways — what a sight! One of the most fantastic sights I have ever seen...

"August 17 ... It was an eight-mile paddle to Helen Falls. We followed the map carefully, as once we neared the falls we had to be close on the left shore to avoid getting into trouble with rapids and falls...

"Gorgeous water falls, with a spectacular force of water rushing over in two areas — a drop of about 40 feet. We found Eric Morse's cairn [built by John Kelsall in 1951], basically the traditional pile of rocks, which was located at the top of the steep hill up which we carried all our gear. He had told us of the tin can which he had put in it with a message in 1962. Since then people passing by had added their own messages. It was fun to read some of them — the tin was jammed full. We wrote our own message — John composed, I wrote — a basic descriptive message with date, route, names and ages (of kids) and place of residence, ending with, 'And oh, the bugs!'..."

Sheila Hoare Thomson (with a Canoe Arctic group led by Alex Hall)
from Hoare Lake to Beverly Lake, 1978.

"I hoped that we might see migrating caribou, but I never dreamed that we would have the great good fortune of watching tens of thousands of caribou streaming past us for an entire day. The glimpses of the tundra wolf chasing caribou, stalking Canada geese, foraging along the shore, and the beautiful white wolf that inspected our camp one morning were revealing snatches of life on the tundra. Seeing the big honey-coloured grizzly asleep beside his musk-ox kill on shore was a thrilling climax to a great trip. For me, however, the highlight of the trip was the visit to my father's old cabin on the Thelon. I could feel his presence there."

Alex Hall on the Thelon River

No one alive knows the Thelon River better than Alex Hall. He has paddled down it at least 30 times over the past 25 years. The love affair began in 1971, when he and a fellow biologist followed in the steps of Eric Morse, Orris Herfindahl, George Rossbach, Keith Acheson and a handful of others. Hall and his partner Ron Thorpe were the eleventh group to canoe down the Hanbury-Thelon strictly for pleasure, since Morse's 1962 trip. Shortly thereafter, Hall started a business, hoping to attract people who wanted to see the Thelon Game Sanctuary by canoe, at least partly driven by his own desire to return again and again.

I remember once being camped along the Thelon with Hall and a group of his clients, when a German couple in an inflatable canoe happened by. It was late in the day, so Rudi and Ingrid were getting anxious to find a campsite. Alex Hall began his description of the next good campsite on downstream and gave them explicit, precise directions that opened with: "Watch for the next gravel bar on your right ..." and went on from there. They could not possibly miss it. Nor did they, a fact we discovered a few days later when we met again and they profusely thanked Hall for sending them to such a beautiful spot. It is beautiful, but that is another story.* The point here is the detailed knowledge of the river embodied in Alex Hall. He could, and did, do the same for any stretch of the Thelon you might care to pick. He knows it better than most people know the neighbourhood they live in. He knows its every turn, its headlands, its gravel bars, its beaches, its overlooks. He carries maps but almost never gets them out. The one time he did in my presence, I noticed

* See the description of the "waterfall glade" in Appendix IV.

something: they are the original maps that he carried in 1971, on his first trip. They have been on every trip since, and are now covered with scrawled notations. What kind of a man could be driven to know one particular river valley so well?

When Alex Hall was a young boy in the 1950s, he and his father had secret fishing spots north of Huntsville, Ontario. "We'd just wade into the creeks up to our waists and fish with a bamboo pole," he remembers. They could, he claims, pull out all the speckled trout they wanted. Their biggest fear, recalls Hall, was that someone would follow them and find out about their secret spots. So they parked their truck — "always a green truck" — well off the road, then used a pine bough to wipe off the tracks on the road shoulder, and hid the truck with a few branches. "Then we'd bushwack into our stream." Knowing this, it is hardly surprising that, as a young adult, Alex Hall sought out a remote, personally special place. Nor is it surprising, as his knowledge of the barrenlands has grown, that he has accumulated a number of "secret" routes and "secret" spots. He is serious about this; enough so that he swears his clients to secrecy on some routes and the locations of wolf-den sites.

Hall has a special affection for wolves. As a Masters student at the University of Toronto in 1970, he was writing up his thesis on the wolves of Algonquin Park, when some fellow graduate students invited him to join them on a field trip researching the wolves of central Baffin Island. "But I'd seen their pictures," he says, "and it didn't look like there'd be anything of interest to me up there." He went anyway, "since it was a freebie." That was his introduction to the Arctic. "It hit me like a sack of bricks." He had to see more, and that led to his 1971 canoe trip down the Hanbury-Thelon.

On the Thelon since, he has come to know the wolves like so many old friends. Every summer he visits a number of dens, and keeps careful records of their occupation. Since Ernie Kuyt left the sanctuary after his wolf work through the sixties, nobody else has studied those wolves more thoroughly than Hall. It is hard to believe, but it is true: Alex Hall communicates with the wolves. I have watched him approach a den, quietly, not with fear but with respect. When the moment is right, he puts his head back and lets out a howl so convincing that any wolf in the neighbourhood probably stops dead in its tracks, and any wolf inside the den comes out to inspect. His stories are legionary of interactions with wolf pups and their parents: about holding young pups in his arms; about running along an esker with the pups, while the mother loped alongside him, apparently enjoying the sport, showing no sign of anxiety or aggression. He exudes respect, even love, for the wolves, but not a whit of fear. A lot of people choose to travel with him just so they too can enjoy the wolves; there is no question, standing face-to-face with an arctic wolf is an unforgettable experience.

Mark Bayer

Alex Hall holding a wolf pup at a den along the banks of the Thelon River, 1989

Hall says it is not unusual to see 10 to 20 wolves while paddling through the treed section of the Thelon valley called the Oasis. They are not, however, at every den every year, and even now after all these years, he still spots new den sites from time to time. After a visit to the first wolf den Hall found on the Thelon in 1971, he recalled that it had been active, with pups, in 11 of the 18 years he had visited, before being flooded out during a high-water year in the early 1990s. "I've had lots of good experiences with the wolves here," he reminisced as we left.

"There's only one thing gets this man excited," said Al Harriot, now in his seventies, who has travelled north to canoe with Hall for many years. "Wolves."

As I watch Alex Hall in the back of his 20-foot Tripper, his short, choppy strokes like bursting explosions of energy propelling the canoe, he appears unflappable. Always in the lead, Hall maintains an easy-going, steady, but unquestioned authority over his clients. He is highly organized and structured — "In the bottom of this pack, I know the sugar's on the left, the milk powder in the centre, the flour on the right, and it stays that way." He exudes confidence, rightly so, and yet never seems domineering. He knows his job, to feed and to lead, and he gets on with it quietly. Most clients, it seems, go away feeling privileged to have shared his insight into the game sanctuary.

It is not just the wolves that draw Hall back to the Thelon time and again, although he admits that if it were not for the wildlife in general, the place would not have its hold on him. "I spend every waking moment just peering around for wildlife," he admitted. "That's all I'm interested in when I'm out there, is looking for wildlife. And there's lots of it to be seen."

Hall believes he may have been the first white man to see a moose in the sanctuary, on his second trip through in 1974. Like Bryan Gordon and Ernie Kuyt before him, he had previously seen signs of moose, but in 1974 about five kilometres upstream from Lookout Point, he spotted a bull moose. Since then, his moose sightings have grown rapidly, most often concentrated in the section of river between the Hanbury-Thelon junction and Hornby Point. In 1977, Hall saw nine moose along that stretch, which leads him to the conclusion that there was "a sudden increase in moose in the Oasis during the early to mid-1970s." As recently as the summer of 1992, he set a new personal record, seeing 19 moose along the Thelon. That same summer, near Warden's Grove, I saw a cow moose with two calves, a relatively rare sighting which is, however, an acknowledged sign of good breeding range.

All of this attention to detail — he has documented all his wildlife sightings, literally thousands of animals, on more than 30 trips down the river — is simply another indication of Hall's attachment to the Thelon. It is "like a mistress," he confesses. The key difference is, he is eager to share the river he loves with others. "I couldn't conduct my business without the Thelon," he admits. "I probably earn 50% of my annual salary out in the Thelon Game Sanctuary." Nonetheless, it has a greater meaning, even to the man who earns his living there. "It's much more than a place where I make my living. It's sacred ground. If I found a billion dollars worth of gold on the Thelon, I would not stake it and I would not tell anyone about it." He wants others to appreciate the sanctuary's value, hoping that somehow it will be preserved as a wilderness forever. In 1986, when the federal government announced a "mineral policy review" that would consider opening the sanctuary to mineral exploration, it was Alex Hall that rallied the troops and led the passionate outcry that resulted in a decision to leave the sanctuary untouched, at least for the time being. Hall, to be sure, is keeping a watchful eye.

When John Hornby's great-nephew wrote to Alex Hall, having seen a Canoe Arctic ad somewhere, to ask if he knew anything about the Thelon, Hall fired off his reply with confidence. "You've got the right man!" wrote Hall in his letter. The result was that Tom Hornby Hill joined one of Alex Hall's trips in 1984, and along the way, spent two solitary hours at the site where his great-uncle perished nearly 60 years earlier.

Over the years that Canoe Arctic has operated, Hall has introduced several hundred other people to the Thelon wilderness. They have come there for many reasons. Most have gone away with indelible memories of wildlife, a feeling of awe for the depth of this wilderness, and an appreciation for Alex Hall's living connection to the river. Many have been drawn to the Thelon over the years, over the centuries, but none more compellingly than this man.

"Being there, in the Thelon, is something akin to a religious experience for me," says Hall. "There's not a day all winter long that I don't think of the barrens. I think that wild country out there is my religion, my church. I worship it. It has taught me the meaning of life. My soul is there. It is the great love of my life. My ashes will go there eventually, so I can be at rest with my true love forever."

13

A Sanctuary for the Future?

We are left with two, closely related questions. What has become of the Thelon Game Sanctuary? What is to become of the Thelon Game Sanctuary? The first thing to note is that it is now more properly called the Thelon Wildlife Sanctuary.

When the sanctuary was originally established by an Order In Council in 1927*, it enclosed an area of about 39,000 square kilometres, within which all hunting by both Natives and non-Natives was prohibited. The primary motive was the conservation of musk-ox, but the intent was to benefit all wildlife, as clarified five years later in a government memorandum: "the supposition that the Sanctuary was created for the express purpose of protecting muskoxen is erroneous, as the preservation of the caribou in this district was equally important in the minds of those who dealt with the question."

There was another problem as well. The prospecting party of Wilson and Dewar *et al.*, which canoed through the sanctuary in 1928, shot and killed a musk-ox for food, faced as they were with severe hunger. This led government to think that travel in the sanctuary, and particularly mining exploration, must be carefully controlled if the ban on hunting were to be effective. So in 1930 a second Order In Council* withdrew the lands of the Thelon Game Sanctuary from "disposal," meaning that prospecting permits and mining claims could not be issued for the area.

In fact, they went even further. A newspaper clipping that survives today inside Christian's original diary — presumably placed there by his parents — is entitled "GAME SANCTUARY - Where No Man May Go." It explains a "ban imposed as result of Hornby

* See Appendix VIII.

tragedy," which will require anyone wishing to enter the Thelon Game Sanctuary to seek written authority from the Canadian Minister of the Interior.

Responsibility for wildlife management and the sanctuary was transferred to the territorial government in 1948, but nothing in effect changed, except that it became necessary to obtain a license from that government prior to entering the Thelon Game Sanctuary. Biologists like John Kelsall and Ernie Kuyt were granted these licenses. Prospectors were not.

Pressure from mining interests continued. In 1956, the NWT Game Ordinance was amended to change the boundaries of the sanctuary. In effect, the western portion of the sanctuary was exchanged for increases in area to the north and southeast. The end result was that the sanctuary grew to a size of 56,000 square kilometres, roughly the size of Nova Scotia. The changes were eventually reflected in a new Order In Council in 1972*, to replace the old one from 1930. Hunting and prospecting within the sanctuary remained illegal.

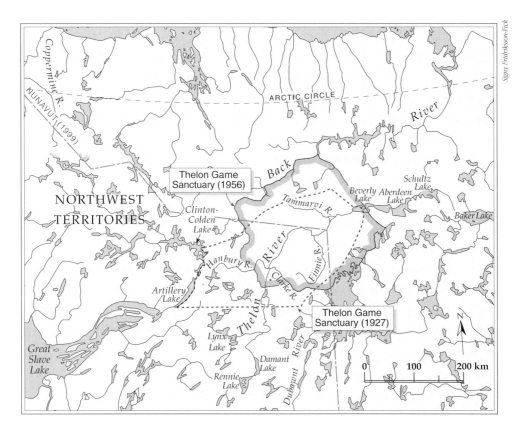

A comparison of the original (1927) and 1956 boundaries of the Thelon Game Sanctuary

See Appendix VIII - Legislation Establishing the Thelon Game Sanctuary

In 1978, the NWT government passed a new Wildlife Ordinance which said, in part, that "No person shall hunt in, commence to hunt in or continue to hunt into a wildlife sanctuary." At the same time, it eliminated the need to obtain a license simply to enter the sanctuary, which made access for recreational canoeists that much easier. This status of the Thelon Wildlife Sanctuary was reiterated when the NWT government passed the current NWT Wildlife Act.

There has been no legislative change in the NWT affecting the sanctuary since that time. Hunting by both Natives and non-Natives remains illegal (although the Native view would challenge this), as does the issuing of surface leases, prospecting and oil exploration permits.

In 1986, when the federal Department of Indian Affairs and Northern Development unveiled its Northern Mineral Policy, it called for a "review of resource utilization in the Thelon Game Sanctuary." It took a while for the word to spread, so low-key was the announcement. But when it did, there was an immense public reaction. According to an official in DIAND at the time, "No one here anticipated anything like this. It was completely unexpected and it's unsettled just about everybody connected to the issue." Conservation groups like the Canadian Nature Federation, the NWT Wildlife Federation, the Canadian Arctic Resources Committee, the Canadian Parks and Wilderness Society, and the Canadian Wildlife Federation all spoke out against any opening of the sanctuary to mineral exploration. None was more effective than a singular Alex Hall, who wrote to Ministers and the committee struck to study the proposal, and rallied dozens of other paddlers from around the world to do the same. It worked. The decision was announced in 1990 that there would be no change to the Thelon Wildlife Sanctuary's boundaries or status.

At the time, Jim Bourque, a Métis who has been active in wildlife management in the NWT for decades, was the Deputy Minister of Renewable Resources. He wanted to see the boundaries expanded, stating firmly that the Thelon was not the place for mineral development, however necessary it might be elsewhere in the NWT. "This is one of the few places in the Canadian North where wildlife can live free of any threat from man, and reproduce without having to deal with machinery or man-made noise. It's like a wildlife bank for us."

It is worth asking just how effective the Thelon Wildlife Sanctuary has been in that role. Since musk-ox were of primary importance in the decision to establish the sanctuary, where, we might ask, is that population now? When the sanctuary was created, it was generally believed that the musk-ox population on the North American mainland had been reduced to only a few hundred, composed of two distinct herds, one of which was centred near the Thelon. Billy Hoare, the first warden of the Game Sanctuary, estimated the Thelon herd's population at 250.

Dr. Clarke, a few years later, upped that to 300. Dr. Kelsall, in 1951, put the figure at about one thousand, although that was later disputed, and in the 1960s biologists believed the musk-ox population in the sanctuary was about 600. More recently, in a 1994 aerial survey, conservative estimates suggest the Thelon now supports at least 1,100 musk-oxen. Alex Hall disagrees, saying "there are at least two to three thousand musk-ox in the sanctuary and possibly many more." The truth probably lies somewhere in between. The important point is that the sanctuary concept has worked. The musk-ox population has grown significantly over the years. In fact, it has grown more than these figures would suggest, because in the last few years experienced travellers of all stripes — Native hunters, canoeists, trappers, biologists — have been seeing more musk-oxen beyond the boundaries of the sanctuary, particularly to the southeast toward the Kazan and the southwest around the headwaters of the Thelon. This evidence suggests that the "herd" within the sanctuary is providing a surplus of animals to repopulate previously abandoned areas of the barrenlands. The far-sighted men who created the Thelon Game Sanctuary in 1927 could not have hoped for better.

———◆———

That story only accounts for the musk-ox. A similar tale could be told of caribou, grizzly bears, wolves, moose and even small mammals like red fox, otter and beaver. The Beverly caribou herd migrates undisturbed to and from its calving ground through the Thelon Wildlife Sanctuary; its population has now grown to more than 300,000. Peregrine falcons, once endangered, nest there in peace. Thousands upon thousands of Canada geese collect there for the period of their summer moult. Tundra swans seem very specific in their selection of the Thelon Oasis section of the sanctuary for their summer breeding. About 50 species of birds nest in the sanctuary every year. Several additional birds — 17 species according to Alex Hall — occasionally extend their range northward beyond their otherwise "normal" limits, in order to nest in the sanctuary.

A "wildlife bank" indeed, and for nearly 70 years a most effective one. The natural balance in the barrenlands' ecosystem had not been disturbed by the indigenous peoples' traditional way of life. So when the sanctuary was created, the ecosystem was essentially "pure." When white man arrived in the North, bringing for his own and for Native use an increasing array of intrusive technology, the Thelon Wildlife Sanctuary enjoyed relative immunity from those incursions. It has remained that way, evolving as it should, largely undisturbed by humans. The result is, we all — Native and non-Native — are the inheritors of one of the world's few untouched wilderness areas. Some feel it has intrinsic value as wilderness itself. Biologists value it as a natural laboratory where nature has been allowed to evolve undisturbed. Hunters outside the sanctuary benefit from its role as a wildlife bank.

What will come of it? If the public reaction in the late 1980s to DIAND's mineral policy review is anything to judge by, many people wish the sanctuary would remain untouched, as it has been. The actual decisions will, of course, be made by those empowered to manage the land in the future. And one can never be certain of what that future holds.

Increasingly, the managers of northern lands will be the Native peoples. That they have an unblemished history as good stewards of the land and its resources — one could say as the original environmentalists — is not a question. But there are new pressures.

At this time, in 1996, new land management discussions are underway as a result of the Nunavut land claim settlement. The border carving the new territory of Nunavut out of the old NWT cuts right through the heart of the Thelon Wildlife Sanctuary, crossing the river just downstream of Lookout Point. The Inuit have established the Akiliniq Planning Committee to oversee the preparation of a management plan for the portion of the sanctuary which lies within Nunavut. Efforts are being made to co-operate in this task with the Dene from Lutsel K'e (Snowdrift) who represent the Native interest for the smaller, western portion of the sanctuary. They have established the Thelon Dezzeth Planning Committee.

The question that remains unanswered is, how do they feel about the Thelon Wildlife Sanctuary? A few years ago, Native organizations — both Inuit and Dene — were uniformly opposed to the possibility of mining in the sanctuary. During the mineral policy review, Tagak Curley, a long-time Inuit leader, placed such importance on retaining the sanctuary that he said "the future of the North is at stake." He expressed concern that Inuit should safeguard their reputation as a people who care about the environment and the wildlife. In today's political climate, however, there is a certain currency to the notion that it is an Aboriginal right to hunt throughout Nunavut, including within the sanctuary. It comes down to a confrontation between the legislation already in force concerning the Thelon Wildlife Sanctuary, and the newly acquired rights under the 1993 Nunavut land claim agreement. Where this debate will lead remains uncertain.

According to Edwin Evo of Qamanittuaq, former chairman of the Akiliniq Planning Committee — in a discussion before the writing of the new management plan began — many Inuit want to see the sanctuary opened for seasonal hunting for domestic purposes, during the winter only. The reality, of course, is that only the most dedicated hunters and trappers will travel that far from home, but there is something of a principle involved in their thinking. At the same time, he expressed genuine concern for the number of birds that nest there, the denning wolves, the caribou migratory paths, and so on — "To conserve all those," said Evo, "it's got to be seasonal hunting, not all year round."

If it can remain a sanctuary under these circumstances, his colleagues prefer to leave it as such. Otherwise, he said, "we may have to think about making it a Park." (It is already an axiom that Native people retain hunting rights, on a non-interference basis, in northern parks.)

As for the Dene, with a proprietary interest in the western portion of the sanctuary, according to Evo who has met with them to discuss a co-operative approach, "the Dene are thinking of following the Inuit decision." The elders of Lutsel K'e do indeed want to see a joint management regime established for the two sectors of the sanctuary, but most Dene favour open hunting all year round, so there is something of a contentious issue yet to be resolved. But Evo is adamant that Inuit and Dene are working together comfortably on this.

As if to prove the feasibility of that suggestion, men and women from each of Lutsel K'e and Qamanittuaq met in the sanctuary for three days in August 1995. A half-dozen or so elders from each community, plus representatives of the two planning committees, camped together on a beach downstream from Warden's Grove, near The Gap, the high hills which force the river into a narrow passage before the wide stretch of water around Grassy Island.

One can imagine the scene. When 85-year-old Zepp Casaway spoke, a younger Dene translated his words into English. Then the Inuit translator repeated it all in Inuktitut, so that David Mannik, 77, and others could understand. Communication, though not easy, was heartfelt.

In one of the opening prayers, Zepp Casaway reminded everyone that the land is the Creator's and implored them not to "give it away." Early in the discussions that followed, Morris Lockhart, another elder from Lutsel K'e, stated the Dene position.

"Our main aim for coming [to this meeting] is to protect the land and to work together [with Inuit] so we can continue to use the land. This land is our land — we must set up rules and policies so white people cannot overuse or destroy it, which would impact our lifestyle. The hunting restrictions did not come from us; they were imposed by the white man. In the sanctuary, food sources are in abundance. Because of the white man's rules, we are restricted from using abundant food sources. This aspect of the sanctuary should be ammended."

Noel Drybone, also from Lutsel K'e, added "As Aboriginal people, we should use the land as we did before the sanctuary was established. I do not want to see development, particularly mining. We have no use for mining which destroys the land. We really love the land and must keep it pure. It is not every day we [Dene and Inuit] meet and talk like this. We should voice a strong statement because it is our land." Other Dene spoke along much the same lines.

Underlying all their statements was a resentment that their people were not consulted when the sanctuary was created in 1927. "The sanctuary was established without consultation," said Pierre Catholique, 68, from Lutsel K'e. "Now we have the opportunity to say how the sanctuary will be managed."

The Inuit are not so immutable nor so strident. While they agree that the sanctuary was unfairly and unilaterally created by white man, there is some measure of recognition in Qamanittuaq for its value today. After all, times have changed, even for the Native peoples. While traditional hunting — before the sanctuary — may well have been non-intrusive, hunting today with heavy-duty snowmobiles and high-powered rifles is not the same thing.

"I have not hunted near the sanctuary," said Inuit elder David Mannik, "but I would be very happy if my grandchildren were able to hunt within it. I am happy that we as elders are talking about the sanctuary and that there is agreement on the major points. I understand that Inuit and Dene hunted in the same area and shared the land. Inuit worked very hard to feed and clothe their families and I know that Dene people had to do the same. Your people have gone through the same harsh times that we have. We have accomplished our goal with Nunavut but we do not want to see our land impacted by development because it destroys the habitat of animals we use. I would like to see my grandchildren take part in the management of the sanctuary."

After two days of talking, David Aglukark, vice-chair of the Akiliniq Planning Committee, said "It is important to have something on paper which we can go back to at a later time," echoing Morris Lockhart's earlier words, "Let's all sign a paper on our common goals."

As the paper was being prepared, a simple hand-written statement of common goals, a moose walked along the beach in front of camp. At a table beside the river, everyone signed the sheet of paper and shook hands all round. For the rest of the evening and on into the night, both Dene and Inuit took turns dancing to the beat of a traditional Dene drum in a circle around the fire.

That there was a sense of community and shared purpose is clear. Where it will lead is much less certain.

If the hunting restrictions were to be lifted, even just for subsistence hunting, the argument would inevitably be made by mining interests that the area no longer has any special status, and should therefore be opened up to mineral exploration. To permit hunting may be to open a Pandora's box in the middle of the sanctuary, setting all the human ills loose in there, leaving us only with hope.

The decision on whether to take that risk, in the end, will fall to the Native peoples. Management of the land has gone full circle. A hundred years ago, no white man had ever been there. In the interim, we have tried to assert our management regime, thus far with noteworthy success in this particular case. But the Thelon is one of the few great wilderness

David Toolooktook (left) and Lawrence Catholique (right) shake hands after signing the paper

Inuit & Dene celebrate together on the banks of the Thelon River

STATEMENT OF INTENT FROM THE INUIT OF NUNAVUT AND DENE FROM ŁUTSELKE REGARDING THE MANAGEMENT PLAN FOR THE THELON GAME SANCTUARY DURING THE HISTORIC' MEETING BETWEEN THE ELDERS OF BAKER LAKE AND THE DENE OF ŁUTSELK'E ON AUGUST 8,9 & 10, 1995

FROM THE DISCUSSIONS, EVIDENCE AROSE OF STRONG LAND USE AND OCCUPANCY WITHIN THE BOUNDARY OF THE THELON GAME SANCTUARY. THE INUIT OF NUNAVUT AND DENE OF ŁUTSELK'E USED THESE LANDS FOR SURVIVAL BY HUNTING, TRAPPING AND FISHING IN THE PRESENT BOUNDARY OF THE THELON GAME SANCTUARY. FURTHERMORE, THE INUIT AND DENE HAVE EVIDENCE THAT THEY HAVE STRONG CULTURAL AND SPIRITUAL TIES WHICH INCLUDE BURIAL SITES AND ARCHAEOLOGICAL SITES WITHIN THE THELON GAME SANCTUARY.

FOR THESE REASONS, THE INUIT AND DENE WISH TO USE THIS MEETING TO FIND WAYS TO COOPERATE WITH EACH OTHER IN DEVELOPING A MANAGEMENT PLAN FOR PRESERVATION, PROTECTION AND USE OF THE THELON GAME SANCTUARY. THE MANAGEMENT PLAN WHICH WILL BE DEVELOPED HAS TO BE SENSITIVE TO THE NEEDS AND WISHES OF BOTH THE INUIT AND DENE. THE MANAGEMENT DOES NOT INFRINGE ON ANY RIGHT OF BOTH PEOPLE.

areas left at this juncture, as we turn its management over to the descendants of its original inhabitants, the people who lived there in workable harmony with the land. How the new generations of Inuit and Dene will tackle the challenge before them remains to be seen.

All of this will be unscrambled in the near future. In 1996 the long-awaited management plan for the Thelon Wildlife Sanctuary will be prepared — a process that will involve public consultation with the Dene of Lutsel K'e, the Inuit of Qamanittuaq, and interested members of the public across Canada. To some extent, this is a recognition that the Thelon Wildlife Sanctuary is of national importance.

The management plan will seek to meet the conservation objectives established by the Akiliniq Planning Committee, and the Thelon Dezzeth Planning Committee of Lutsel K'e, all of which goals offer ample reason to feel optimistic about the future of this pocket of wilderness. As events unfold over the next few years, we will see how the Native people deal with this regained responsibility, but the early indications are that they will be able to strike an appropriate balance between conservation and exploitation.

14

A River, A Beginning

The river carries us downward to its conclusion, and at the same time bears us upward to new levels of understanding.

As I paddle, stroke after stroke, down the length of the Thelon, past familiar spots that somehow look different every time I pass, the river sometimes speaks to me. The voice is soft and subtle. Its words are hidden in the rocks and sand and spruce alongside the river, or deep beneath the glassy surface in the fluid heart of the river itself. I have to listen for them, to look for them, or they can easily pass unheard. They speak of the mystery. They talk of rebirth. They address the unspoken questions embodied in every canoeist who comes here.

To the extent that the river has become the centre of my life on this trip, it will answer those questions that I have brought to it. It will bear me up to a new level of understanding — understanding of this wilderness, of humanity, of myself, this sanctum. And yet I will never have all the answers. I know this, for the urge to return will never go away. If I am comfortable in this state, then I have accepted the river, and it has accepted me. It is my river.

There have been others before me, of course: a few hundred non-Natives, like myself, in the course of the last century. And before that countless numbers of Native people, who came here on their own quests, most often in search of food and survival. For everyone, in some manner, the river valley held the answers they sought. Some do not recognize them. Others, the lucky ones, do. With all of us, having sought and found, the river has forged a personal link. We have our own connection. It is our river.

Just as the river is not discriminatory in whom it benefits, we must all share in its care. It is *our* river. Natives and non-Natives alike, having converged from different responsibilities, different histories, different quests, now share this responsibility. There is a certain irony, a certain correctness, and a certain inevitability in the fact that it is the Native peoples who now hold the balance of power in the management of this wilderness. That is how it was a hundred years ago, and now the land has been through the colonial cycle of European influence and come out once again under the jurisdiction of the Native peoples. One hopes they have the wisdom of their forefathers. But we all, everyone of us who goes there or even cares to know it exists, share in the responsibility of stewardship. It is our river.

It was David Hanbury and J.W. Tyrrell's river, when they went there to cross the frontier of white man's knowledge, to explore and to chart new lands. It was John Hornby's river when he went there to prove something to himself. It was the trappers' river when they went there to find a life of independence and self-reliance in the Country. It was young Edgar Christian's river when he went there to become a man, and succeeded, and died in doing so. It was Billy Hoare and Jack Knox's river when they went there to do a job and to meet every challenge it put before them. It was C.H.D. Clarke's river when he went there to record its bio-diversity. It was John Kelsall's river when he went there in search of caribou. It was Ernie Kuyt's river, in ways unprecedented, when he lived on its banks and studied its wolves and falcons. It was Eric Morse's river when he went, in his understated way, in search of "a different holiday, spiced with just enough risk to border on adventure." It was Alex Hall's river when he first found it, fell in love, and it is his again every time he returns, as it will be again some day, he says, in death. It is my river. It is your river.

For the Inuit who once used the Thelon valley upstream of Beverly Lake, it was a source of wood. They were a pragmatic people. Perhaps the river then lacked any spiritual proportion, but today among the Inuit of Qamanittuaq it has gained the stature of legend.

For the Dene of Lutsel K'e (Snowdrift), it is still a living memory. Zepp Casaway was a young hunter in the 1930s, but he remembers: "I have been in the barrenlands, away up to a place called the Thelon River. I was there for 12 years, trapping. That area is really beautiful. There are all kinds of animals there, all different kinds. I lived in that area very good when I was young. For food, when we went out, if we have tobacco, matches, gun, shells, flour, sugar, tea, and oats, if we have that then we're okay for out in the barrenlands."

It is their river.

For every one of these people, from James W. Tyrrell to Alex Hall, for Pingawalook and Telaruk, for Thanadelthur and Casaway, the Thelon held a special mystery of some sort. It has manifested that power in different ways at different times for each person who has known it. In a way, the Thelon defines us as Canadians: Inuit, Dene, or non-Native — we all can feel a connection to this land. No other northern river has a history like the Thelon's.

No other river has drawn such a range of travellers to it. No other river has produced such legends. Only the Thelon.

The mystery of the Thelon will never really be solved. It cannot be. That is the very quality that allows its allure to endure, to draw me and others back time and again, so that our canoes can drift through a land still untouched, where the mystery of wilderness is allowed to abide, to touch our lives.

Perhaps, like the central mysteries of life itself, the Thelon is best explained by reference to God, or the Great Spirit, or whatever you wish to call the ultimate power. That was the Chipewyan solution, whose Dene descendants repeatedly refer to the Thelon as the place "where God began when the world was created." And so, to understand the Thelon as best we can, we are left to seek some answer in the wisdom of the Native people who knew it first. If the world began there, how did it happen?

This is an old Chipewyan story of creation, as told in 1863 by Ekounelyel, a blind old man at Great Bear Lake, and repeated by Dene through the years in many versions.

In the beginning there were no people on Earth. Then, suddenly, they say, Man appeared. As winter approached, the first man, Ttathe Dene, wanted to make something — snowshoes, without doubt. "How am I going to do it?" he wondered.

Having cut some birch, he made the frame of the snowshoes. The next day, after having dried them, he put in the cross-piece. The third day, he finished them except for the webbing which would cover them. "Alas, how shall I weave them?" he wondered.

That was impossible for him to do because it was woman's work and there was no woman. He then left his snowshoes unfinished in the tipi, and lay down discouraged, for he had not found a way to weave the webbing. When night came he fell asleep. The next day when he awoke, the first man found that one of his snowshoes was half-strung. "Who has come to string my snowshoes during my sleep?" asked the man.

When evening came, he lay down again and when day came the snowshoe was fully strung. Then raising his eyes to the top of his tipi, he saw a snow ptarmigan flying outside the tipi. "Ah! That ptarmigan must be the one that has helped me," said the man.

The sixth night the snowshoes were all finished, and the ptarmigan flew away again. "I know what to do to catch this ptarmigan," said Dene. On awakening the next day, he saw his snowshoes beside him and the ptarmigan ready to escape; but he closed the opening of the tipi, and the ptarmigan, finding herself trapped, changed into a beautiful woman.

And so they married and became the parents of many men and women. And we are those men, because we are truly men from the beginning.

The Inuit, too, have their stories of creation, passed down in the oral tradition from generation to generation. The first Inuit, they say, emerged from the ground, coming up as hummocks of earth or tussocks of grass, and then turning into a man and a woman. And that was the beginning.

The Thelon, still today, is the place where all men and women can go to be as close as possible to the beginning. The untouched pocket we call the Thelon Wildlife Sanctuary is the purest wilderness left in continental North America. In our approach to the 21st century, it is a sanctum.

As I dip my paddle once again into its waters, and look down into the river's dark secrets, I can see only a hint of the power that this place holds. I know that it has set me free. I move on inexorably, and the water once parted by my canoe folds back into itself. I leave the river alone, free to continue on toward its destiny.

Appendices

Appendix I:
Chronology of Known Journeys through the Thelon Valley

It must be acknowledged here, as elsewhere in the book, that prior to the white man's arrival in the Thelon valley, Native people had travelled up, down, and across the river valley for thousands of years.

1893 - J.B. Tyrrell and J.W. Tyrrell, having descended the Dubawnt River, joined the Thelon at Beverly Lake and followed it out to Hudson Bay.

1899 - David T. Hanbury, canoed upstream from Chesterfield Inlet to the headwaters of the Hanbury and over the divide to Great Slave Lake.

1900 - J.W. Tyrrell, canoed down the Hanbury-Thelon to Beverly Lake, and then back up the upper Thelon above the junction as far as the confluence of the Elk River, then walked overland to Artillery Lake.

1901/02 - David T. Hanbury descended the Hanbury-Thelon by canoe to Baker Lake, where he overwintered, then travelled back upstream by dog-sled to Beverly Lake, where he headed overland to the arctic coast.

1908 - RNWMP Inspector E.A. Pelletier, accompanied by three other Mounties, descended the Hanbury-Thelon, having started in Great Slave Lake, to finish at Chesterfield Inlet.

1911 - Harry V. Radford & Thomas George Street, descended the Hanbury-Thelon, overwintered at Schultz Lake, and in the spring of 1912 travelled overland with Inuit to Bathurst Inlet, where they were both killed. Radford mounted the expedition to study musk-oxen, with a view to collection, for American Museums. He hired Street at Smith's Landing (now Fort Fitzgerald) and the two travelled alone from Fort Resolution eastward to the Thelon in an 18 1/2 foot cedar strip canoe. At Schultz Lake, they hired Akulack and a second man for the overland trip. The two white men were killed at Bathurst Inlet after Radford provoked a fight with local Inuit men who refused to accompany him further.

In 1917 the RNWMP sent a patrol from Baker Lake to investigate the murders. Inspector F.H. French and Sergeant-Major T.B. Caulkin travelled 5,153 miles in a ten-month period. In their version of events, when Radford and Street wanted to move on from

Bathurst Inlet in June of 1912, "at the last minute one of [the local Inuit guides] changed his mind because his wife was sick having been hurt in a fall. Radford tried to force the man and took a dog whip to him. Street attempted to restrain Radford but Radford beat the Eskimo and then dragged him to the edge of the ice and open water. The others were afraid that Radford would throw the man into the water so they attacked him and speared him to death. Street had run to his sled where the rifles were but the Natives overtook him and killed him with their snow knives." It was the policemen's conclusion that "the Eskimos had been provoked and had acted in a spirit of self-defence." No arrests were made.

A few months later, Billy Hoare, early in his career, before coming to the Thelon country, met one of the murderers, Amigainuk. The Inuk became his friend and travelling companion along the arctic coast. For two years they shared the trials and tribulations of travel in the Arctic. When they parted, Amigainuk gave Hoare a matched set of white fox furs to take south for Street's family in Ottawa, as something of an apology for having murdered Street.

1925 - John Hornby and James Critchell-Bullock canoed down the Hanbury-Thelon.

1926 - John Hornby, Harold Adlard, Edgar Christian followed the Hanbury-Thelon to a site where they built a cabin to overwinter, now known as Hornby Point.

1928 - Harold S. Wilson, Ken M. Dewar, John B. Muirhead and John Thomson, as a prospecting party, canoed down the Hanbury-Thelon to Baker Lake.

1928/29 - W.H.B. "Billy" Hoare & Jack Knox travelled in to the Thelon country, back and forth to Reliance, to establish the camp at Warden's Grove, and then canoed downriver to Baker Lake.

1929 - Hjalmar Dale (a.k.a. Hjalmar Nelson) travelled from Lynx Lake to Baker Lake by homemade canoe.

1929 - RCMP patrol canoed into the Hornby cabin from Fort Reliance: Inspector Charles Trundle, Cpl. R.A. Williams, Const. E.A. Kirk and Const. M.E. Bobblets

1930/31 - Billy Hoare, travelled by small frieghter canoe from Baker Lake up to Aberdeen Lake, and as far up the Thelon as the confluence of the Tammarvi River.

1936 - Col. Harry Snyder led an American expedition, the "Barren Ground Expedition," which flew into the Game Sanctuary to observe and photograph musk-oxen. Steel Lake, north of Warden's Grove, is named after the Canadian government observer on the flights, Col. F.M. Steel.

1936/37 - C.H.D. Clarke and Billy Hoare travelled the sanctuary extensively, engaged in biological surveys by air, by freighter canoe and in the final summer by paddle down the Hanbury-Thelon to Baker Lake.

1948 - J.B. Bird in a party of four led a geological exploration by canoe of the lower Thelon.

1951 - John Kelsall and Nolan Perret, canoed from the Hanbury junction down to Baker Lake, on Canadian Wildlife Service duty surveying caribou and musk-oxen.

1952 - John S. Tener, Mammalogist with the Canadian Wildlife Service, and Dr. John E. Bardach, professor of biology at Iowa State Teachers College conducted a musk-ox study by canoe from Grassy Island to Beverly Lake.

1954/55 - The initial "official" mapping of the Thelon valley by the Geological Survey of Canada — part of an ambitious project commenced in 1952 to complete the geological map of 57,000 square miles of the Precambrian Shield, lying west of Hudson Bay—used helicopters and aerial surveys over much of the lower Thelon country.

1962 - The first purely recreational canoe trip across the Barrens, from Sifton Lake down the Hanbury-Thelon to Baker Lake, was led by Eric Morse, with his wife Pamela, Arch Jones and Bill Nicholls. This was the beginning of a new era.

Appendix II:
Gazeteer of the Thelon Valley

Aberdeen Lake - named by J.B. Tyrrell in 1893 after his friend and supporter, the Governor General of Canada, Lord Aberdeen.

Abbott Lake - near the headwaters of the Hanbury River, named by David Hanbury in 1899 "after my friend and old travelling companion in Central Asia, Dr. W.L. Abbott."

Akiliniq - Inuktitut for "that which lies above" referring to a ridge of hills along the north side of Beverly Lake.

Ark-i-linik River - the name used by David Hanbury for the Thelon, taken from the Inuit name Akiliniq.

Baker Lake - the lake at the mouth of the Thelon River, connected to Hudson Bay by Chesterfield Inlet, so-named in 1762 by the first white explorer, William Christopher, after Sir William Baker, Governor of the Hudson's Bay Company. The Inuit community situated here is called Baker Lake in English and Qamanittuaq in Inuktitut, meaning "where the river widens into a lake."

Beverly Lake - (also Tivialik in Inuktitut) named by James W. Tyrrell in 1900 after Beverly Fairchild, the son of Tyrrell's assistant, C.C. Fairchild.

Clarke River - a tributary joining the Thelon just before the confluence with the Hanbury, named after the biologist Dr. C.H.D. Clarke.

Cosmos Lake - named in 1978 by Operation Morning Light, designating the site where the largest pieces of the Soviet satellite Cosmos 954 crashed to Earth.

Deville Lake - near the headwaters of the Hanbury River, named by James W. Tyrrell in 1900 after "our worthy surveyor general," Dr. E.G. Deville.

Dickson Canyon - on the Hanbury River, named by James W. Tyrrell in 1900.

Douglas Lake - near the headwaters of the Hanbury River, named by James W. Tyrrell in 1900 "after my own little boy."

Eyeberry Lake - on the Thelon River, named by James W. Tyrrell in 1900 "because of the abundance of eye-berries which we found on its shores and islands."

Finnie River - a tributary of the Thelon, joining at Lookout Point, named in 1925 by John Hornby and James Critchell-Bullock after O.S. Finnie, head of the North-West Territories and Yukon Branch of the Department of the Interior, in Ottawa, 1922-31. (see Appendix IV)

Ford Falls - on the Hanbury River, named by James W. Tyrrell in 1900.

Grassy Island - on the Thelon River, 20km downstream from the Hanbury junction, named by James W. Tyrrell in 1900 "because of the growth of grass covering it, upon which musk oxen were observed to be feeding."

Hanbury Lake - a small lake, next downstream from Lac du Bois on the Hanbury River, named by H.V. Radford and T.G. Street in 1911, after David Hanbury.

Hanbury River - named after David Hanbury, first white man to travel it (in 1899, upstream), by James W. Tyrrell, who descended it the following year.

Helen Falls - on the Hanbury River, named by James W. Tyrrell in 1900 after his daughter. (see Appendix IV)

Hoare Lake - the last lake on the Hanbury before the river enters the fast-flowing run (including Dickson Canyon) down to join the Thelon, named after W.H.B. "Billy" Hoare.

Hoare Point - the point at the mouth of the Thelon, on the east side of the river as it enters Beverly Lake, where Billy Hoare built a warden's cabin in 1931. (see page 72)

Hornby Point - originally referred to as Hornby's Bend, commemorating the site where John Hornby and two companions died in 1927. (see Appendix IV)

Kaninguaq - local Inuit name for the lower Thelon, including the stretch from Schultz Lake down to Baker Lake.

Lac du Bois - on the Hanbury River, downstream from Sifton Lake, named by James W. Tyrrell in 1900 "from the occurrence on its shores of a few thinly scattered spruce trees."

Lookout Point - named by James W. Tyrrell in 1900, no doubt because this raised headland offers sweeping views in many directions. (see Appendix IV)

Macdonald Falls - on the Hanbury River, named by James W. Tyrrell in 1900.

Mary Frances River - a tributary to the Thelon River, named by James W. Tyrrell in 1900 after his wife (also Mary Frances Lake, the headwaters of the river).

Muskox Hill - beside Sifton Lake, near the headwaters of the Hanbury River, named by James W. Tyrrell in 1900 after a successful muskox hunt. (see page 21)

Muskox Hill - a pingo just east of the Thelon River, about 20km upstream from Lookout Point, so named in recent years because numbers of musk-oxen were often seen in the vicinty. (see Appendix IV)

Oasis - although the Thelon Oasis is not an official name, it is widely used to describe the well treed section of the river valley from Warden's Grove down to just below Hornby Point. In this area in particular, there is a rich diversity of plant and animal life.

Sandy Lake - on the Hanbury River, downstream from Sifton Lake, named by James W. Tyrrell in 1900 "because of the very remarkable and high white sand hills to the north of it, and its white sand shores and bottom."

Schultz Lake - named by J.B. Tyrrell in 1893 after the Lieutenant Governor of Manitoba, Sir John Schultz.

Sifton Lake - near the headwaters of the Hanbury River, named by James W. Tyrrell in 1900 "in honour of the Minister of the Interior," Clifford Sifton.

Smart Lake - near the headwaters of the Hanbury River, named by James W. Tyrrell in 1900.

Steel Lake - north of Warden's Grove, named after Col. F.M. Steel, the Canadian government observer on the 1936 "Barren Ground Expedition," which flew into the Game Sanctuary to observe and photograph musk-oxen.

Tammarvi River - a tributary joining the Thelon at Ursus Islands, which takes its name from the Inuktitut for "wrong way," presumably referring to earlier journeys from Beverly Lake taken by Inuit travelling upstream in search of trees.

The Gap - named by James W. Tyrrell in 1900, probably because on approach, it appears that the river is obstructed, but just at the last minute, "a gap" opens up to allow passage downstream.

Thelon - a corruption of the Chipewyan name for the river, the The-lew-dezeth. (also variously Teh-lon-diseth, Thlewy-dezza, Thlew-y-aza, and Teh-lon), probably meaning "Fish River."

Ti-bi-elik - see Tivialik

Tivialik - an Inuit name meaning "the place of drifted wood" referring to the area of Beverly Lake.

Tyrrell Lake - on the Mary Frances River, a tributary to the Thelon River, named by James W. Tyrrell in 1900 after himself, "since I am sure it has never been, and perhaps never will be, of as much interest to any one else as it proved to me."

Ursus Islands - name proposed by biologist Ernie Kuyt after he spent the summer based there in 1960. There have been reports of sighting large numbers of grizzly bears in this area.

Warden's Grove - although not an official name, it is in widespread use, referring to the stand of spruce where Billy Hoare and Jack Knox built their cabin in 1928, just downstream from the Hanbury-Thelon confluence. (see Appendix IV)

Appendix III:
If You Go — A Canoeist's Guide

Access: It is possible to approach the headwaters of either the Thelon or the Hanbury by canoe. The Hanbury is by far the most popular among those eschewing the fly-in option. The portage into the headwaters of the Hanbury is a relatively short one from the bottom of Clinton-Colden Lake.

Chartering a float-plane out of either Yellowknife or Fort Smith, one can conveniently begin a trip at Lynx Lake on the Thelon or on the Hanbury at either Sifton or Campbell Lake. There are, of course, innumerable options in the upper reaches of both branches. On either branch there are some substantial portages.

There are a number of air charter operators, and they change frequently, so it is best to get an up-to-date list (phone the Northwest Territories Travel Information office in Yellowknife at 1-800-661-0788) and then make enquiries regarding airplane capacity, range, and costs directly with the charter companies. Some summers it is possible to originate an air charter out of Baker Lake, which allows you to paddle back to your point of embarkation.

Some people like to begin their trip near the Hanbury-Thelon junction, in order to avoid long portages. In this case, the best landing for a float-plane is likely found on the Hanbury, just a few miles above the junction, downstream of Helen Falls. Starting here allows one to spend the first day or two hiking up the Hanbury, to view Helen Falls and Dickson Canyon.

It is quite possible to paddle from the Hanbury-Thelon junction to Baker Lake with only one portage, around the rapids at the outlet from Schultz Lake (by which time the load of food is almost negligible).

Paddling Through the Sanctuary:

The paddle from the Hanbury-Thelon junction to Beverly Lake is easy, with current most of the way and only some minor riffles to deal with. The highlights here are provided by the wildlife. You will almost certainly see musk-oxen. You stand a good chance of seeing caribou, moose, wolf and grizzly bear. There are usually several raptors nesting along the cliffs lining the river through "the big bend" between Hornby Point and Lookout Point. You will pass several interesting archaeological and historical sites.

While it would be possible to do it in less, approximately 12 days is the recommended minimum for this stretch across the breadth of the Sanctuary. Allow more if you can, to permit side-trips and exploration on foot.

Egress: Paddling all the way down to Baker Lake is, of course, a popular option because regularly scheduled flights are available there. In this case allow plenty of extra time for difficult and potentially dangerous crossings of the large bodies of open water (Beverly, Aberdeen and Schultz Lakes).

For those who (wisely) would like to avoid the big lakes, a charter flight out from the point where the Thelon enters Beverly (back to Yellowknife or Fort Smith) is a most satisfying, albeit expensive, option. There is a good spot for a pre-arranged pick-up at the last bend in the river, just 7 km upstream from the rivermouth: good camping, deep water, good beach, adequate shelter.

It is possible to arrange in advance to be picked up by boat, in which case you must co-ordinate with someone from the community of Qamanittuaq (Baker Lake), on date, location, etc.

Once you reach Baker Lake, a community well worth a visit of several days, you have to deal with the problem of your canoes. It is possible but costly to ship them out, normally. It is also possible to sell them locally, but of course it is a buyer's market so don't expect to get full value. If you are planning a return to the barrenlands in a subsequent summer, it is quite easy to make local arrangements for the canoes to be stored over-winter. For more information on Baker Lake, contact the Tourism Officer at 819-793-2992.

Archaeological Sites:

All canoeists are asked to remember that the archaeological artifacts found on the barrenlands are the property of those Native people who descend from the original manufacturers. It is not only illegal, but also immoral, to remove any artifact. Admire the signs you will see of former human presence, but leave them undisturbed.

Appendix IV:
Some Places of Interest in the Wildlife Sanctuary

(in order, travelling downstream)

Helen Falls, Hanbury R. - on river left, the east bank, there is a cairn, built in 1951 by John Kelsall and Nolan Perret, who were working for the Canadian Wildlife Service on a survey of caribou and musk-ox in the Game Sanctuary. Their note was later removed and mailed to the Ottawa headquarters of the C.W.S. The oldest note extant was deposited by Eric Morse and his party in 1962.

Warden's Grove - Established by W.H.B. "Billy" Hoare and Jack Knox in 1928 as the headquarters for the Warden of the Thelon Game Sanctuary. They built the two older cabins, set back in the stand of spruce, one for storage, the other to live in. In 1961, the trapper Fred Riddle was hired by the Canadian Wildlife Service (for whom he worked as a "Predator Control Officer," poisoning wolves) to build a new cabin. Sitting right at the edge of the spruce grove, this cabin is just visible from the river, on the left (north) bank about 10 km downstream from the Hanbury-Thelon junction.

The cabin has been used by various parties since:

1970,71	- summer headquarters for Bryan Gordon's Upper Thelon Archaeological Project (plus occasional years thereafter up to 1984).
1972	- summer headquarters for a musk-ox wool gathering project.
1977/78	- six adventurers, including Chris Norment and Robert Common, overwintered there, part of an expedition to commemorate the anniversary of Hornby's death.
1989,90,91	- summer headquarters for Chris Norment's study of Harris' sparrows, the basis for his PhD.
1992	- my last visit before the writing of this book, for ten days, hiking the surrounding country, hoping (in vain) to watch the annual caribou migration which usually passes southward somewhere nearby in mid-July, and on which occasion I repaired a major collapse of the roof. The cabin itself was in good condition.

Waterfall Glade - on river right about 20 km upstream from Hornby Point, there is a gravel bed extending out slightly into the river. It is the first such gravel bed downstream (about 6 km) from a narrows where the river often generates a slight riffle. It makes for a good lunch-stop, or a passable campsite, though not as good as beside the aforementioned narrows. Behind the gravel bed, even from the river, you can just see a thin waterfall dropping down to the level of the Thelon from the plain above. In the small glade around the pool at the foot of the waterfall, there appears to be a microclimate which supports the growth of several species of plant not usually found this far north, including raspberry, currant, and columbine.

Cairn - On the end of a point extending upriver, on river right (south bank) just 400 metres downstream from the waterfall glade above, there is a tall, rock cairn, built by Ernie Kuyt and his wife Elsie, while they were camped there in the summer of 1963.

Hornby Point - originally referred to as Hornby's Bend, the site of John Hornby's legendary tragedy. The ruins of the actual cabin where he and two younger companions lived and died are somewhat upstream of the point, and the graves of John Hornby, Harold Adlard and Edgar Christian, each marked with a wooden cross, are right beside the cabin. The cabin site can be difficult to find, hidden in the woods on the left (north) bank. This sketch map, taken from one of my trip journals, should help.

The site is approximately one kilometre back upstream from the actual point. The rocky shore of the point leads back into a marshy area, where the spruce are noticeably farther inland from the solid green shoreline. Continuing upstream, another exposed gravel bank is visible for about 75 metres, but it again gives way to 100 metres of thickly willowed riverbank between the river and the forest. Upstream from that, there is a rocky bank (of varying width) extending for nearly a kilometre on upstream. Near the downstream end of this long rocky bank, where there are actually willows growing right along the shore below the gravel bank, Hornby's cabin and the graves are only about 30 metres back into the woods. In their time (1926), it was less thickly wooded, and the cabin enjoyed a view over the river, facing south.

In trying to follow this description, remember that water levels fluctuate considerably from year to year, and from the beginning of summer to the end. Furthermore, the gravel banks are rearranged somewhat by the ice every year.

There is quite a good campsite across the river, on the south side, mid-way between the cabin and the point, hidden behind an ice-pushed boulder bank.

Muskox Hill - about 20 km upstream from Lookout Point, on river left (east bank) but not visible from the river because it is some distance inland, is the first, and for some time only, pingo known to be in the Thelon Game Sanctuary. It is well worth the hike inland from the Thelon River to visit Muskox Hill.

Pingo is an Inuit word meaning "a round hill." That is just what it looks like, a perfect dome rising out of the flat tundra. In this case, as you draw nearer, especially if the evening light happens to be low, it takes on a golden hue as the sand on top is burnished by

Paul vonBatch

The Thelon pingo

the sun. A fellow canoeist, having walked in to see it, once called it "a golden temple." I've seen it look reddish, when wet, and a pinkish buff when baked dry. Every time the colour seems to change.

Pingos, most commonly found around the Mackenzie Delta, normally stand where a lake used to be. Surrounded by permafrost, the lake drained; in time the residual water contained within the lake-bed froze and expanded upward into a dome-shaped hill, often surrounded by a ring of water. The hill remains covered with the lake's sand and till, but its core is still ice.

The Thelon pingo, uniquely situated so far inland, is in an old channel of the river. It was noticed by a scientist in 1954 flying over the area, and visited the following year by a geologist. He found that the layer on top of the ice core, composed almost entirely of silt and no sand, contained some organic remains. These were tested in a laboratory and determined to date back approximately 5500 years, suggesting that the area was at that time forested, and subject to repeated spring flooding. Now, of course, the river has cut its present valley deep enough that it no longer floods into the pingo. These clues lead to the conclusion that the pingo was formed more recently than 5500 years ago, probably caused by the same climatic cooling that lead to the retreat of the forest.

Falcon Creek - Ernie Kuyt's name for a small tributary entering the Thelon just downstream from Muskox Hill. On the bank of this creek, in the 1960s, Kuyt found a roll of birchbark in an old campsite. He concluded that it must have been dropped there by someone, probably a Dene hunter from farther south, assuming that it could not have floated *up* the creek from the river. It looked to have been worked by human hands, evidenced by puncture holes. He collected it and forwarded it to the National Museum, where it was identified as a rogan, a type of water-carrying vessel.

Finnie River - In the early 1960s, biologist Ernie Kuyt found a number of tree stumps in a clearing a short distance upriver from the Thelon, evidence, he says, of "Eskimo logging" to make sled runners. According to Kuyt, "you could see the cuttings on the trees, some of them 16 inches at the butt, and the tops still lying there."

On a map drawn by Pukerluk for Knud Rasmussen, during his Fifth Thule Expedition 1921-24, the Inuk indicated a tributary that corresponds with the Finnie River and labelled the area around it as "aklajet." Rasmussen's notes interpret that as a "timbered district with a tributary, favourite place of land bears."

A short paddle up the Finnie is worthwhile, if only to see the pocket of rich growth, including tamarack and several unusual plants.

Lookout Point - It is worth stopping here to climb up for the view up and down the valley. In addition, there are several archaeological remnants on top of the hill, indicating that Native people used this location. Artifacts found here and nearby have been assessed as Inuit, Chipewyan and Arctic Small Tool Tradition.

Crossing Place of Deer - Named after a notation on James W. Tyrrell's map, presumably the translation of a Native name, although there are several other places along the Thelon where larger numbers of migrating caribou cross. It was here (just downstream from 102°W, at a distinct bend to the east) in 1951, atop a drumlin on the river's left bank, that John Kelsall erected a stake with the following inscription:

J.P. Kelsall - N.G. Perret - Can. Wild. Ser. - Aug. 2 '51.

Appendix V:
Letter from J.C. Critchell-Bullock to Colonel W.F. Christian

45 EATON PLACE,

S. W. 1.

SLOANE 7448.

1 October 1937.

Col. W. F. Christian, D.S.O.,
Bron Dirion,
Caernarvon.

Dear Colonel Christian;

        I have read UNFLINCHING with great
interest. It is of course a document that will
rightly find its place in every public library in
the land. It must have taken some courage on your
part to have decided to deal with it as you have.
I should like to congratulate you, if I may...

        As I write, I have before me two
letters from the Commission of the Mounted Police
which read in part as follows, and are dated
12th. October 1928 and 10th. April 1929 respect-
ively: "on account of damage to the seaplane
and the wrecking of the attendant schooner, it
will now be impossible to make the desired patrol
of the Hornby Cabin. It will be some months
before I shall get any further details." Then:
"The Non-Commissioned Officer who intended to
make the patrol to the Hornby Cabin was brought
out from Reliance suffering from appendicitis,
and it is now the intention to patrol to the
cabin by the first open water." So they also
had a rough time.

        It may interest you to know that I had
information that, when the trio met the Indians
and whitemen on Great Slave Lake when going in,
their canoe contained only one sack of flour,
a small quantity of pemmican, sugar and tea, and
that they obtained the rest of their supplies by
chance from the Stewart Brothers, who had a cache
at the east end of the Lake. I should judge, from
my own experience of Hornby, and from what I have
heard about their final equipment, that their
supplies consisted of three sacks of flour, one
and a half of sugar, a couple of slabs of bacon,
and oddments such as tea.

To me of course it is inconceivable that
Hornby should have attempted to "live off" that
country again, while the extremely narrow escape
that he and I had must have been fresh in his
memory. On occasions we were reduced to living on
meat that looked more like molasses than flesh,and
was literally swimming in maggots.

I made three trips with Hornby altogether;
two of them short, but on all three we came close
to starvation, even when within a couple of days
walk of a township. He utterly despised, for some
reason, Government expeditions, Police patrols, and
any party that went into the country with a view
to avoiding hardship. That was why other old-
timers were scared of travelling with him.

Anybody thoroughly understanding Hornby,
as you did, could hardly condemn him for this
tragic business. Even I have often felt my flesh
creep at the thought of what he must have suffered
mentally when he had to face up to the inevitable.
The pride of the man was so immense, and his
affection for your son was,from what friends who
met them both have told me, so real that the whole
show must have been torture.

Undoubtedly neither of the youngsters
suffered as he did, from that standpoint. Men
living as they were for almost a year become
amazingly hardened to hardship. If I tried to eat
putrid fermenting fish today it would poison me.
It hardly phazed me then. The same applies to
living conditions, environment, and the squalor of
it. Dump off the toughest product of civilization
into those conditions, and he would not last a
week. Starvation becomes an everyday event, and
the: "let's hope for better luck tomorrow" a mechan-
ical utterance. Their emaciated bodies would be
hardly noticeable to themselves, and creaking joints
a topic for conversation. You go on and on, becoming
weaker and weaker, and the worse you become the less
your faculties register.

I remember once in 1923, on my first
trip with Hornby, remarking on how queer I felt and
asking why. Hornby's reply was: "Well, you're
starving, you know." He of course was starving, too,
but semi-skeleton though he must have been, I noticed
nothing strange in his appearance.

Another point: Hornby and I used to scrap a bit between ourselves; but that was when we had the energy to scrap on. When it became touch and go, there was no trouble. If there had been, there would have been a killing.

Hornby should never have taken Adlard, whom I knew well. Adlard wanted to come with us, and Hornby would have taken him, but for the fact that I put my foot down. He was a first class lad, but only in civilization. The opinion of some people was that a crash he had with the R.A.F. had affected him. But considering everything, it appears that his hunting was more productive than the others'. He was a good shot I recollect.

No, it was a happy thing that both young men were so loyal to Hornby, and that it was their first trip with him. I think I can assure you that your son's attitude towards what was eventually inevitable must have been peaceful in comparison to what you or I would have suffered had we suddenly been dumped off there to die say in two or three weeks. I remember that (excluding my miserable Christmas alone in our cave when I made "preparations") there was an occasion half way down Thelon River when Hornby and I faced up to facts and chatted over the possibility (or probability) of leaving our bones where we were. (We were so weak that we could not climb out of our canoes to put up a mosquito net on the river bank. A chance wolf saved us.) I am sure that, if either of us was anxious, I must have been more nervy than Hornby, but I clearly remember that I wrapped up, sealed and tinned, my records and films, as though it were the most normal thing in the world to do, and without the least sign of jitters. Too hardened to it, too fagged out.

Yours sincerely,

[signature]

Appendix VI:
Mammals of the Thelon Valley

Brown lemming   *Lemmus sibiricus*

Collared lemming   *Dicrostonyx torquatus*

Red squirrel   *Tamiasciurus hudsonicus*

Ermine   *Mustela erminea*

Arctic ground squirrel (sik-sik)   *Spermophilus undulatus*

Arctic hare   *Lepus arcticus*

Arctic fox   *Alopex lagopus*

Red fox   *Vulpes vulpes*

Wolverine   *Gulo gulo*

Arctic wolf   *Canis lupus hudsonius*

Barren-ground caribou   *Rangifer tarandus*

Moose   *Alces alces*

Muskox   *Ovibus moschetus*

Grizzly bear   *Ursus arctos*

Appendix VII:
Birds of the Thelon Valley

Gaviidae

Common loon	*Gavia immer*
Pacific (Arctic) loon	*Gavia pacifica*
Red-throated loon	*Gavia stellata*
Yellow-billed loon	*Gavia adamsii*

Anatidae

Whistling Swan	*Cygnus columbianus*
Canada goose	*Branta canadensis*
White-fronted goose	*Anser albifrons*
Snow goose	*Chen caerulescens*
Black duck	*Anas rubripes*
Northern Pintail	*Anas acuta*
Green-winged teal	*Anas carolinensis*
American Wigeon	*Anas americana*
Lesser Scaup	*Aythya affinis*
Greater Scaup	*Aythya marila*
Oldsquaw	*Clangula hyemalis*
White-winged Scoter	*Mellamitta deglandi*
Common Merganser	*Mergus merganser*
Red-breasted Merganser	*Mergus serrator*

Accipitridae

Rough-legged hawk	*Buteo lagopus*
Golden eagle	*Aquila chrysaetos*
Bald eagle	*Haliacetus leucocephalus*
Northern harrier	*Circus cyaneus*

Falconidae

Gyrfalcon	*Falco rusticolus*
Peregrine falcon	*Falco peregrinus*
Merlin	*Falco columbarius*

Tetraonidae
Willow ptarmigan   *Lagopus lagopus*
Rock ptarmigan   *Lagopus mutus*

Gruidae
Sandhill crane   *Grus canadensis*

Charadriidae
Semipalmated plover   *Charadrius semipalmatus*
Lesser Golden plover   *Pluvalis dominica*

Scolopacidae
Semipalmated sandpiper   *Ereunetes pusillus*
Least sandpiper   *Erolia bairdii*
Spotted sandpiper   *Actitis macularia*
Stilt sandpiper   *Calidris himantopus*
Common snipe   *Copella gallinago*
Lesser yellowlegs   *Tringa flavipes*

Phalaropodidae
Red-necked phalarope   *Phalaropus lobatus*

Stercorariidae
Long-tailed jaeger   *Stercorarius longicaudis*
Parasitic jaeger   *Stercorarius parasiticus*

Laridae
Herring gull   *Larus argentatus*
Bonaparte's gull   *Larus philadelphia*
Mew gull   *Larus canus*
Arctic tern   *Sterna paradisaea*

Strigidae
Snowy owl   *Nyctea scandiaca*
Short-eared owl   *Asio flammeus*

Alaudidae
Horned lark   *Eremophila alpestris*

Hirundinidae
Cliff swallow   *Petrochelidon pyrrhonota*

Corvidae
Gray jay   *Perisoreus canadensis*
Common raven   *Corvus corvax*
Turidae
American robin   *Turdus migratorius*
Gray-cheeked thrush   *Catharus minimus*

Laniidae
Northern shrike   *Lanius excubitor*

Montacilidae
Water pipit   *Anthus spinoletta*

Emberizidae
Blackpoll warbler   *Dendroica straita*
Hoary redpoll   *Acanthis hornemanni*
Common redpoll   *Acanthis flammae*
Savannah sparrow   *Passerculus sandwichensis*
Tree sparrow   *Spizella arborea*
Harris' sparrow   *Zonotrichia querula*
White-crowned sparrow   *Zonotrichia leucophrys*
White-throated sparrow   *Zonotrichia albicollis*
White-winged crossbill   *Loxia leucoptera*
Lapland longspur   *Calcarius lapponicus*
Snow bunting   *Plectrophenax nivalis*

Appendix VIII:
Legislation Establishing the Thelon Game Sanctuary

AT THE GOVERNMENT HOUSE AT OTTAWA

Wednesday, the 15ᵗʰ day of June, 1927

PRESENT:

HIS EXCELLENCY

THE GOVERNOR GENERAL IN COUNCIL

WHEREAS the Minister of the Interior represents that recent explorations in the Mackenzie and Keewatin Districts of the North West Territories indicate that there are only two small herds of muskox left on the mainland, one of which ranges in the vicinity of the Hanbury and Thelon rivers;

That it is reported that some years ago there were many musk-ox in these districts, but owing to the gradual encroachment of white trappers and hunters armed with modern firearms, there is grave danger of them being exterminated;

That the Game Regulations of the North West Territories provide that no person shall hunt, trap, take, kill, shoot at, wound, injure, or molest musk-ox at any time of the year;

That owing to the difficulty of enforcing a regulation of this nature in so large and remote an area, the Advisory Board on Wild Life Protection and the Director of the North West Territories are of opinion that it would be in the interest of conservation of wild life in general and musk-ox in particular to create a game sanctuary in the area in question;

That it is further reported that there are no trading posts or permanent residents, either white or native, in the area proposed to be set aside, and that the country is unsuited for agriculture;

THEREFORE His Excellency the Governor General in Council, on the recommendation of the Minister of the Interior, and under and in virtue of the provisions of sub-section 10(h) of Section 4 of the North West Game

Act, as amended by Chapter 60, 10 - 11 George V, an Act to amend the North West Game Act, 1st July, 1920, is pleased to order that the hereinafter described area be and it is hereby created a game sanctuary as from the 1st September, 1927, viz:

"Commencing at the point on the southerly shore of Beverly lake where the left bank of Dubawnt river intersects the said southerly shore; thence south-westerly, following the height of land between the Dubawnt and Thelon rivers to its intersection with the sixty-third (63) parallel of north latitude; thence due west following the said sixty-third (63) parallel of north latitude to its intersection with the east shore of Artillery lake; thence northerly following the east shores of Artillery lake, Ptarmigan lake, and Clinton-Colden lake and connecting waterways to the sixty-fourth (64) parallel of north latitude; thence due east along the said sixty-fourth (64) parallel of north latitude to its intersection with the height of land between the waters of the Thelon and Back rivers; thence north-easterly following the said height of land to the portage between the Buchanan and Tibielik rivers; thence south-easterly following the west bank of the Tibielik river to Beverly lake; thence following the north shore of said lake to a point due north of the point of commencement; thence due south to the said point of commencement, containing an area of approximately fifteen thousand (15,000) square miles."

His Excellency in Council is hereby further pleased to order that the said area be placed, for the purposes of administration, under the jurisdiction of the North West Territories and Yukon Branch of the Department of the Interior.

[signature]

approved

[signature] Willingdon

15. 6. 77.

AT THE GOVERNMENT HOUSE AT OTTAWA

TUESDAY, the 4th day of FEBRUARY, 1930.

PRESENT:

HIS EXCELLENCY

THE GOVERNOR GENERAL IN COUNCIL:

WHEREAS by an Order in Council dated the 15th day of June, 1927, (P.C. 1146) a tract of land in the Northwest Territories known as the Thelon Game Sanctuary was set apart for the conservation of wild life;

AND WHEREAS the Minister of the Interior reports that this object will not be attained if prospectors are permitted right of entry upon the said game sanctuary;

AND WHEREAS the Deputy Minister of Mines states that the geological conditions of the area included in the said game sanctuary appear to be less favourable than other parts of the surrounding region and that its remoteness from any railway or steamship route would be a handicap to mining development;

THEREFORE His Excellency the Governor General in Council, on the recommendation of the Minister of the Interior and under and by virtue of the provisions of Section 74(e) of Chapter 113, R.S. 1927, is pleased to order that all the lands comprised in the Thelon Game Sanctuary be and they are hereby withdrawn from disposal under the said Act and reserved for the purposes of wild life conservation.

Ernulapunta

Approved

Willingdon

4. 2. 30

CANADA

PRIVY COUNCIL · CONSEIL PRIVÉ

HIS EXCELLENCY THE GOVERNOR GENERAL IN
COUNCIL, on the recommendation of the Minister of
Indian Affairs and Northern Development, is pleased
hereby, pursuant to section 19 of the Territorial
Lands Act,

(a) to revoke Order in Council P.C.
      233 of 4th February, 1930;

(b) to order the withdrawal from
      disposal under the Act of the
      lands described in the Schedule,
      including the minerals under-
      lying such lands, whether precious,
      base, solid, liquid or gaseous,
      without prejudice to the rights
      of the holders of recorded mineral
      claims in good standing under the
      Canada Mining Regulations or of
      permits or leases in good standing
      under the Canada Oil and Gas Land
      Regulations, for the purpose of a
      game sanctuary; and

(c) to set apart and appropriate the
      lands described in the Schedule
      for such purpose.

Approved — Approuvé

P. M.
The Senate

Deputy Governor — General
Gouverneur general suppléant

24 MAY MAI 1972

Appendix IX:
A Short Geological History of the Thelon Valley

The Thelon River today cuts right across the Canadian Shield, through rocks more than 2,500,000,000 years old — among the oldest on Earth. The rock is mostly granite, sometimes metamorphosed to gneiss. It forms the geological core of the barrenlands, a solid, consistent and uniform foundation. The rock dates back to a time when the continents did not exist as we know them today, when the world was essentially lifeless, when there was much less oxygen in the Earth's atmosphere.

For the next two billion years, rivers and shallow seas flooded over much of the Earth. In the region that one day was to become the Thelon valley, the flooding deposited sandstone and volcanoes erupted to intermingle lava on top of the older bedrock foundation. In the Thelon region today, as a consequence, the surface is composed primarily of this sandstone. In several places in the Thelon basin, flat-lying outcrops of this formation are now evident. The most commonly found sedimentary rock here is a white, or sometimes reddish, coarse-grained sandstone. Bands of conglomerate formed of quartzite pebbles can be seen in the sandstone found in the hills overlooking the Thelon. All of this sedimentary rock dates back more than 1800 million years. In it, there is some fossil evidence of the most rudimentary forms of life existing during this period. But it was not until 1200 million years later that life burst forth. About 200 million years ago, the continents as we know them were formed by the splitting of a single large land mass.

Then the marine cover began to drain away, exposing for the first time the new land. One of the water courses thus established followed what is now roughly the Thelon River. The extension of the Thelon valley is still evident on the floor of Hudson Bay, stretching right across to Hudson Strait. Of the barrenland rivers today, the Thelon is one of few that can be said to have survived from this time of the land's first exposure. By about two million years ago, this process of drainage had produced the rough outline of northern Canada as we know it.

Then began a great Ice Age. There were several glaciations, spanning most of the last two million years of the Earth's history. The most recent was the most important in refining the present landscape. It started about 20,000 years ago. At its maximum, several huge ice sheets covered most of North America, in places to a depth of four kilometres. The Thelon valley, indeed all of the barrenlands, was covered by the Laurentide ice sheet, extending from the Rocky Mountains to Labrador and from the arctic islands south well into the U.S.A.

Geological epochs and events

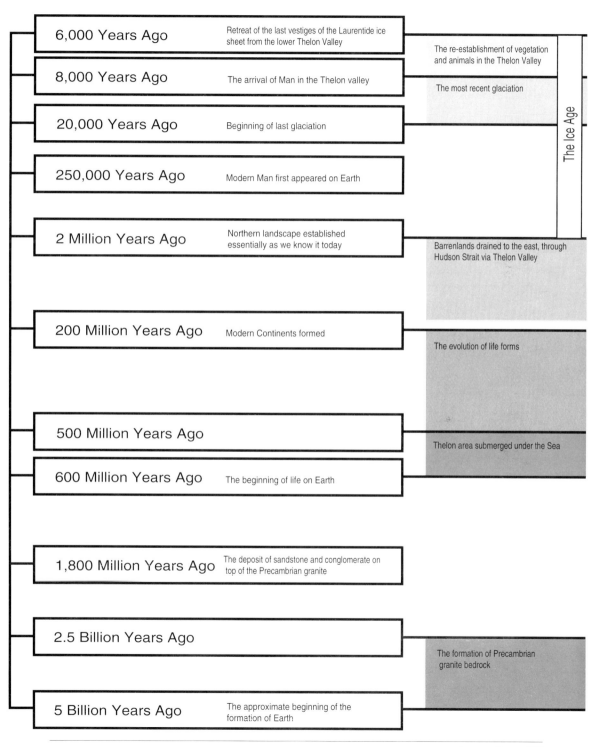

6,000 Years Ago	Retreat of the last vestiges of the Laurentide ice sheet from the lower Thelon Valley
8,000 Years Ago	The arrival of Man in the Thelon valley
20,000 Years Ago	Beginning of last glaciation
250,000 Years Ago	Modern Man first appeared on Earth
2 Million Years Ago	Northern landscape established essentially as we know it today
200 Million Years Ago	Modern Continents formed
500 Million Years Ago	
600 Million Years Ago	The beginning of life on Earth
1,800 Million Years Ago	The deposit of sandstone and conglomerate on top of the Precambrian granite
2.5 Billion Years Ago	
5 Billion Years Ago	The approximate beginning of the formation of Earth

The re-establishment of vegetation and animals in the Thelon Valley

The most recent glaciation

The Ice Age

Barrenlands drained to the east, through Hudson Strait via Thelon Valley

The evolution of life forms

Thelon area submerged under the Sea

The formation of Precambrian granite bedrock

The highest ridge of ice in the Laurentide sheet west of Hudson Bay ran north-south across the Thelon valley. The Keewatin Ice Divide, stretching 700 kilometres from the Manitoba border north to Wager Bay, across the Thelon between Schultz Lake and Baker Lake — from which ice flowed in all directions during glaciation — played a critical role in the latter stages of the Ice Age, as the glacier melted. It provided a dividing line between east and west. Today, its presence is evidenced by the absence of glacial features found to the east and west.

During the expansion and then retreat of the ice, the surface of the landscape was altered once again. The advancing ice scraped off loose material, picked up huge chunks of granite, and ground up solid bedrock to sand and clay. Moving very slowly — perhaps one metre in a year — across the rock surface, armed with these rock tools and weighted down by the thickness of pure ice, the glacier caused erosion and scouring of the granite surface. During the Ice Age, some of the granite bedrock, never before uncovered, was exhumed from beneath the younger sandstone and remains exposed today. The evidence of the glacial action is etched on the polished, striated surfaces of the rock; there are dramatic examples in the Thelon valley. The remnants of volcanic and sedimentary cover also bear the mark of the glaciers. In places, the ice eroded deep valleys, some of which were to become the lakes of the Thelon system. The floors of both Baker and Schultz Lakes were excavated to well below current sea-level.

Millennia later, when the ice melted, all manner of debris was deposited on the newly exposed surface. Huge chunks of bedrock picked up earlier were simply left *in situ* when the ice melted. Till — unsorted, nonstratified sediment from clay to sand to gravel — previously collected under the ice, was sometimes carried out beyond the margins of the ice by the melt waters. Other times it was deposited directly onto the underlying surface as the ice above melted. Although generally less than two metres thick, in places close to the river till accumulated to a depth of more than 30 metres on top of the bedrock; that is why sections of the river are lined with cliffs. In general, these till deposits required only minor rearranging to produce the landscape we see today.

On occasion, the till was moulded by the flow of the ice into a series of parallel cigar-shaped ridges, called drumlins. They can be several miles long and may be anywhere from 5 to 20 metres high. The Thelon basin contains what is probably the largest drumlin field in the world, centred in the area between the Hanbury junction and Beverly Lake.

Inside the ice of the glacier, there was also a collection of sand and gravel. That too was eventually deposited, carried by the flow of melt water, in streams developed mostly under the ice. The sinuous ridges of dry sand and gravel left by these subglacial streams are called eskers. Standing from 5 to 50 metres above the surrounding landscape, they mark the drainage routes once used by water flowing beneath the melting ice sheet. The upper Thelon country, in particular, has large numbers of these eskers, some many miles long. One, in particular, starts just west of Dubawnt Lake, crosses the Thelon about 25 kilometres downstream from Eyeberry Lake, and continues to the northwest for a total distance in excess of 400 kilometres.

As the Laurentide ice sheet shrank, huge amounts of melt water accumulated, barred from flowing to Hudson Bay by remaining glacial ice at the Keewatin Ice Divide. The land flooded, forming what geologists call glacial Lake Thelon. As the perimeter of the glacier continued to retreat, the lake extended eastward, spreading over a larger area, and its level dropped. The lake, more than 200 metres deep in places, eventually encompassed most of the present Thelon and Dubawnt drainage above Aberdeen Lake, an area of roughly 80,000 square kilometres. To this day, the careful observer can see dry beach lines on the hillsides around the river as far downstream as Aberdeen Lake, marking former lake levels. The lake continued to expand eastward — with the resultant drops of water-level — by stages, until finally the water broke through the deteriorating ice sheet, toward the sea to the east.

Then the sea, a much enlarged Hudson Bay (called the Tyrrell Sea), invaded the area where the land had been depressed by the weight of ice, penetrating upstream as far as Lookout Point. All the land to the west of the Keewatin Ice Divide presently below an elevation of 110 metres above modern sea level was flooded. At its maximum extent, the sea occupied this vast basin, leaving only the ground now higher than 110 metres as islands. Since that time, the land has risen and the seashore has gradually shifted to the east. But it, too, left beach lines to mark its former shoreline at each stage of its decline. It is virtually impossible for the amateur — and even for the experienced geologist — to differentiate between the old beach lines of the lake and those of the sea. The marine beaches often contain fossil shells, while the old lake beaches are devoid of any sign of life. Eventually, when the water subsided, the shape of the landscape as we see it today was unveiled.

Fire and ice, earthquakes and floods, winds and oceans had all done their work. On top of the world's oldest rock, the world's youngest landscape lay ready to receive life.

Appendix X:

About The Publisher

*"Canada's Paddling
Information Specialists"*

Founded in 1971 as a result of an individual paddler who was unable to obtain information on a canoe trip being planned to La Ronge in northern Saskatchewan, the Canadian Recreational Canoeing Association (CRCA) has dramatically increased the availability of information to paddlers worldwide on how to experience Canada's waterways. From its early, meagre beginnings, the CRCA has become known across Canada for the many services provided to canoeists, kayakers and sea kayakers.

The Association publishes *KANAWA* Magazine, the voice of paddling in Canada, which is available on a quarterly basis for $20 per year plus 7% GST. (U.S.A. and international orders $20 U.S. per year plus 7% GST.) Other programs and services include liability insurance for instructors, canoe courses offered through provincial/territorial affiliates and canoe clubs, the Bill Mason Memorial Scholarship Fund, National Let's Go Paddling Week, Canadian Canoe Route Environmental Clean Up Project and the Nikon Canadian Canoe Photography Contest, as well as guided canoe and sea kayaking trips through its adventure travel arm, Canada's Canoe Adventures.

The CRCA not only publishes guide books and maps on paddling Canada, but also keeps in inventory the largest collection of material available on paddling in Canada. Call or write for a **Paddling Catalogue**, available free of charge upon request. Before your next paddling adventure, be sure to contact us:

**Canadian Recreational Canoeing Association
1029 Hyde Park Road, Suite 5
Hyde Park (London), Ontario, Canada N0M 1Z0**
Phone (519) 473-2109/641-1261 Fax (519) 473-6560

(Please note that the Association will be moving to its Outdoor Education Centre in Merrickville, Ontario as of September 1996.)

The new address will be:
P.O. Box 5000, 446 Main St. West, Merrickville, Ontario, Canada K0G 1N0.

Other books published by the Canadian Recreational Canoeing Association:

Temagami Canoe Routes	*Missinaibi – Journey To The Northern Sky*
Rivière Dumoine	*Nahanni - River of Gold...River of Dreams*
Rivers of the Upper Ottawa Valley	*Canoeing Canada's Northwest Territories – A Paddler's Guide*

Bibliography

The Land

Aylsworth, J.M. and Shilts, W.W. 1989. *Glacial Features Around the Keewatin Ice Divide: Districts of Mackenzie and Keewatin.* Paper 88-24. Ottawa: Geological Survey of Canada.

Bardach, J.E. 1964. *Downstream: A Natural History of the River.* New York: Harper & Row.

Bird, J.B. 1951. The physiography of the middle and lower Thelon basins. *Geographical Bulletin* 1: 14-29.

———— 1953. The glaciation of central Keewatin, NWT. *American Journal of Science* 251(3): 215-30.

———— 1967. *The physiography of arctic Canada.* Baltimore: Johns Hopkins Press.

———— 1980. *The natural landscapes of Canada.* Toronto: Wiley Publishers of Canada.

Blanchet, G.H. 1930. *Keewatin and Northeastern Mackenzie.* Ottawa: Canada, Dept. of Interior.

Bodden, K. (ed.) 1980. *Regional Analysis of Natural Region 16: Central Tundra.* Edmonton: Boreal Institute for Northern Studies.

Craig, B.G. 1959. Pingo in the Thelon Valley, N.W.T.; radiocarbon age and historical significance of the contained organic material. *Bulletin of Geological Society of America* 70: 509-10.

——— 1964. *Surficial Geology of East-Central District of Mackenzie.* Bulletin no. 99. Ottawa: Geological Survey of Canada.

Dean, W.G. 1953 . The drumlinoid landforms of the "Barren Grounds". *Canadian Geographer* 3: 19-30.

Hiscock, B. 1986. *Tundra, the Arctic Land.* New York: Atheneum.

MacDonald, G. 1991. The Making of the Landscape. In *The Kazan — Journey into an Emerging Land.* Yellowknife: Outcrop.

McGill University, Dept. of Geography, 1963. *A Report on the physical environment of the Thelon River area.* Santa Monica, California: The Rand Corporation.

Wright, G.M. 1967. *Geology of the Southeastern Barren Grounds, Parts of the Districts of Mackenzie & Keewatin.* Memoir 350. Ottawa: Geological Survey of Canada.

Zaslow, M. 1975. *Reading the Rocks — The Story of the Geological Survey of Canada, 1842-1972.* Toronto: Macmillan.

The Native People

Arima, E.Y. 1984. Caribou Eskimo. In *Handbook of North American Indians - Arctic,* ed. D. Damas, 5: 447-62. Washington: Smithsonian Institution.

Birket-Smith, K. 1929. The Caribou Eskimos. *Report of the Fifth Thule Expedition, 1921-24.* vol.5, parts 1 & 2. Copenhagen: Gyldeddalske Boghandel, Nordisk Forlag.

——— 1930. Contributions to Chipewyan Ethnology. *Report of the Fifth Thule Expedition, 1921-24.* vol.6, no.3. Copenhagen: Gyldeddalske Boghandel, Nordisk Forlag.

Burch, E.S. Muskox and Man in the Central Canadian Subarctic, 1689-1974. *Arctic* 30(3): 135-54.

Frison-Roche, R. 1974. *Hunters of the Arctic.* Toronto: J.M. Dent & Sons.

Gillespie, B.C. 1975. Territorial Expansion of the Chipewyan in the 18th Century. In *Proceedings: Northern Athapaskan Conference, 1971,* ed. A.M. Clark. Mercury Series no.27. Ottawa: Canada, National Museum of Man.

————— 1976. Changes in Territory and Technology of the Chipewyan. *Arctic Anthropology* 13(1): 6-11.

Gordon, B.H.C. 1975. *Of Men and Herds in Barrenland Prehistory.* Mercury Series no.28. Ottawa: Archaeological Survey of Canada, National Museum of Man.

————— 1975. 1974 Current Research. *C.A.A. Bulletin.*

————— 1977. Prehistoric Chipewyan Harvesting at a Barrenland Caribou Water Crossing. *The Western Canadian Journal of Anthropology* 7(1): 69-83.

————— 1981. Man-Environment Relationships in Barrenland Prehistory. *Musk-ox* 28:1-19.

Harp, E. 1961. *The Archaeology of the Lower and Middle Thelon, Northwest Territories.* Technical Paper no.8. Montreal: Arctic Institute of North America.

————— 1962. The cultural history of the central barren grounds. In *Prehistoric Cultural Relations bewteen the Arctic and Temperate Zones of North America,* ed. J.W. Campbell. Technical Paper no. 11, pp 69-75. Montreal: Arctic Institute of North America.

Helm, J. 1975. Introduction to the contact history of the subarctic Athapaskans: An Overview. In *Proceedings: Northern Athapaskan Conference, 1971,* ed. A.M. Clark. Mercury Series no.27. Ottawa: Canada, National Museum of Man.

Irving, W.N. 1968. Prehistory - The Barren Grounds. In *Science, History and Hudson Bay,* eds. C.S. Beals and D.A. Shenstone, 1: 26-54. Ottawa: Dept. of Energy, Mines and Resources.

Janes, R. 1973. Indian & Eskimo contact in southern Keewatin: an ethnohistorical approach. *Ethnohistory* 20(1): 39-45.

Jenness, D. 1932. *Indians of Canada.* Bulletin 65, Anthropological Series no.15. Ottawa: Canada, National Museum of Canada.

————— 1956. The Chipewyan Indians: an account by an early explorer. *Anthropologica* 3(1): 15-34.

Parker, J. 1972. The Fur Trade and the Chipewyan Indians. *The Western Canadian Journal of Anthropology* 3(1): 43-57.

Rasmussen, K. 1930. Observations on the Intellectual Culture of the Caribou Eskimos. *Report of the Fifth Thule Expedition, 1921-24.* vol.7, part 2. Copenhagen: Gyldeddalske Boghandel, Nordisk Forlag.

Robinson, J. 1944. Among the Caribou-Eaters. *The Beaver* 275(3): 38-41.

Rogers, E.S. 1970. The Chipewyan. *The Beaver* 301(3): 56-59.

——— 1970. *Indians of the Subarctic.* Toronto: Royal Ontario Museum.

Smith, J.G.E. 1975. The ecological basis of Chipewyan socio territorial organization. In *Proceedings: Northern Athapaskan Conference, 1971.* Mercury Series no.27. Ottawa: Canada, National Museum of Man.

——— 1976. Introduction: The historical and cultural position of the Chipewyan. *Arctic Anthropology* 13(1): 1-5.

——— 1978. Economic Uncertainty in an "Original Affluent Society": Caribou and Caribou Eater Chipewyan Adaptive Strategies. *Arctic Anthropology* 15(1): 68-88.

——— 1984. Chipewyan. In *Handbook of North American Indians - Sub-Arctic,* ed. W.C. Sturtevant, 6: 271-284. Washington: Smithsonian Institution.

Smith, J.G.E. and Burch, E.S. 1979. Chipewyan and Inuit in the Central Canadian Subarctic 1613-1977. *Arctic Anthropology* 16(2): 76-101.

Stewart, A. 1991. Hunters — Life from the Land.
In *The Kazan — Journey into an Emerging Land.* Yellowknife: Outcrop.

Van Kirk, S. 1974. Thanadelthur. *The Beaver* 304(4):40-45.

VanStone, J.W. 1965. *The Changing Culture of Snowdrift Chipewyan.* National Museum of Canada Bulletin 209. Ottawa: Canada, Dept. of the Secretary of State.

Wright, J.V. 1968. Prehistory - The Boreal Forest. In *Science, History and Hudson Bay,* eds. C.S. Beals and D.A. Shenstone, 1:54-68. Ottawa: Dept. of Energy, Mines and Resources.

——— 1972. *The Shield Archaic.* Publications in Archaeology, no.3. Ottawa: National Museums of Canada.

——— 1972. *The Aberdeen Site.* Mercury Series no.2. Ottawa: Archaeological Survey of Canada, National Museum of Man.

The History of Exploration

Baird, P.D. & Robinson J.L. 1945. A brief history of exploration and research in the Canadian Eastern Arctic. *Canadian Geographical Journal* 30:136-57.

———. 1949. Expeditions to the Canadian Arctic. *The Beaver* 279(4): 44-47, 280(1): 41- 47, 280(2): 44-48.

Blanchet, G.H. 1949. Thelewey-aza-yeth. *The Beaver* 280(2): 8-11.

——— 1950. Into Unknown Country. *The Beaver* 281(1): 34-37.

——— 1963. Book Review: *The Legend of John Hornby*. *The Beaver* 293(4): 58.

——— 1963. The Letter. *The Beaver* 293(4): 41-44.

Christian, E. 1937. *Unflinching: A diary of tragic adventure.* London: John Murray Ltd. (Republished with the title *Death in the Barren Ground*, G. Whalley ed., in 1980 by Oberon Press, Ottawa.)

Critchell-Bullock, J.C. 1925. Field work in the lower Arctic zone. *Canadian Field Naturalist* 39: 181-83.

———. 1930. An expedition to sub-arctic Canada, 1924-25. *Canadian Field Naturalist* 44:53-59, 81-87, 111-17, 140-45, 156-62, 187-96, 207-13, and 45:11-18, 31-35.

Hall, H.H. 1913. *Report of trip to the timber on the Thelew [Thelon] River during the summer of 1913.* HBCA RG3/20F/4. Winnipeg: Hudson's Bay Company Archives. (also A.12/FT Misc.107 reel 856 or B401/a/2 reel 1ma14)

Hanbury, D.T. 1900. A Journey from Chesterfield Inlet to Great Slave Lake 1898-99. *Geographical Journal* 16(1): 63-76.

——— 1903. Through the Barren Ground of northeastern Canada to the arctic coast. *Geographical Journal* 22(2): 178-91.

——— 1904. *Sport and Travel in the Northland of Canada.* London: Edward Arnold.

Hearne, S. 1795. *A Journey from Prince of Wales's Fort ... to the Northern Ocean ... in the years 1769, 1770, 1771 and 1772.* London: A. Strahan and T. Cadell.

Hoare, W.H.B. 1990. *Journal of a Barrenlander.* Ottawa: MOM Printing.

Inglis, A. 1978. *Northern Vagabond: The Life and Career of J.B. Tyrrell, the Man who Conquered the Canadian North.* Toronto: McClelland & Stewart.

Mills, E. 1946. James W. Tyrrell, Explorer. *The Beaver* 277(2): 38-41.

Rivett-Carnae, C. 1973. The establishment of the RCMP presence in the NWT and the Arctic. *Canadian Geographical Journal* 86(5): 155-67.

Ross, W.G. 1968. On the Barrens 1934. *The Beaver* 299(2): 48-53.

Seton, E.T. 1908. A canoe trip to the plains of the caribou. *Geographical Journal* 32(3): 275-77.

———— 1911. *The Arctic Prairies.* New York: Harper & Row.

Tyrrell, J.B. 1897. *Report on the Dubawnt, Kazan, and Ferguson Rivers ...* Annual Report for 1896, vol.9, report F: 1-218. Ottawa: Geological Survey of Canada.

Tyrrell, J.W. 1902. Report of an Exploratory Survey between Great Slave Lake and Hudson Bay. *Appendix no.26, Part III, Annual Report 1901.* Ottawa: Dept. of Interior.

———— 1908. *Across the Sub-Arctics of Canada.* Toronto: William Briggs.

———— 1924. *Report on an exploratory survey between Great Slave Lake and Hudson Bay.* (Reprinted from Dept. of Interior *Annual Report, 1901.*) Ottawa: Topographic Survey of Canada.

———— 1942. *Explorations and Adventures in Northern Canada, being the Life Story of James W. Tyrrell, 1882-1942.* (Unpublished ms. in Ontario Archives).

Trundle, C. 1929. *Report on the late John Hornby and Party.* G Division HQ file no.25 D.I.L.G. (Reprinted in Whalley, *Death in the Barren Ground*, 172-80.)

Waldron, M. 1931. *Snowman: John Hornby in the Barrenlands*. Boston: Houghton Mifflin.

Whalley, G. 1962. *The Legend of John Hornby*. London: John Murray.

——— 1969. Notes on a Legend. *Queen's Quarterly* 76(4):613-34.

——— 1980. *Death in the Barren Ground*. Ottawa: Oberon Press.

Wray, O.R. 1934. In the footsteps of Samuel Hearne. *Canadian Geographical Journal* 9(3): 139-46.

The Trappers

Harpelle, A. 1984. *Those were the Days that I Lived and Loved: A biography of Gus D'Aoust*. Steinbach, Manitoba: Martens Printing.

Ingstad, H. 1992. *The Land of Feast and Famine*. Montreal: McGill-Queen's University Press.

Johnson, H. 1979. Recalling the trail amid the trappings of trade. *Edmonton Journal* (March 14).

Lees, N. 1989. The dead men were tough as they come. *Edmonton Journal* (Feb. 19).

The Wildlife

Banfield, A.W.F. 1951. *The barren ground caribou*. Ottawa: Canada, Dept. of Resources and Development.

Bardach, J.E. 1952. Report on the field investigation of the Thelon Game Sanctuary. Canadian Wildlife Service C.W.S.C. 200 (unpublished).

Canadian Nature Federation 1990. Reprieve for Sanctuary. *Almanac* 4(5): 1.

Claricoates, J. 1991. *Thelon River 1991: Report on the Scientific Fieldwork*. Report prepared for the Canadian Wildlife Service, Yellowknife (unpublished).

Clarke, C.H.D. 1940. *A biological investigation of the Thelon Game Sanctuary*. National Museum of Canada Bulletin 96, Biological Series no.25. Ottawa: Canada, Dept. of Mines and Resources.

Goodwin, G.C. 1936. 8,000 Miles of Northern Wilderness. *Natural History* 37: 421-34.

Gray, D.R. 1987. *The Muskoxen of Polar Bear Pass.* Toronto: Fitzhenry & Whiteside.

Hall, A.M. 1976. Encounters with the tundra wolf. *The Beaver* 307(3): 30-35.

Heard, D.C. and Williams, T.M. 1992. Wolf den distribution on migratory caribou ranges in the Northwest Territories. (Paper awaiting publication).

Hoare, W.H.B. 1930. *Conserving Canada's Muskoxen.* Ottawa: Canada, Dept. of Interior.

Hornby, J. 1934. Wildlife in the Thelon River area. *Canadian Field Naturalist* 48(7):105-11.

Kelsall, J.P. 1951. *The Thelon Game Sanctuary - 1951.* Canadian Wildlife Service C.W.S.C. 198 (unpublished).

———- 1953. Biological investigation of the Thelon Game Sanctuary, 1951. *The Arctic Circular* 6(1): 7-8.

———- 1968. *The Migratory Barren-Ground Caribou of Canada.* Ottawa: Queen's Printer.

———- 1972. The northern limits of Moose (*Alces Alces*) in western Canada. *Journal of Mammalogy* 53: 129-38.

Kennedy, J. 1989. *Project Oasis: A report on wildlife observations along the Thelon River, July 21 - August 4, 1989.* Yellowknife: East Wind Arctic Tours.

———- 1990. *Project Oasis II: A report on wildlife observations and other notes of interest of a trip on the Thelon River, July 6-20, 1990.* Yellowknife: East Wind Arctic Tours.

Kuyt, E. 1960. Notes from the Thelon Game Sanctuary, N.W.T. *Blue Jay* 18(3): 103.

———- 1962. Movements of young wolves in the Northwest Territories of Canada. *Journal of Mammalogy* 43(2): 270-1.

———- 1962. Northward dispersion of banded Canada geese. *Canadian Field Naturalist* 76: 180-1.

―――― 1965. Three mammal records from the Thelon Game Sanctuary, N.W.T. *Blue Jay* 23(3): 134-5.

―――― 1965. Additional notes on recent occurrence of mammals in the Thelon Game Sanctuary, N.W.T. *Blue Jay* 23(4): 173.

―――― 1972. *Food Habits and Ecology of Wolves on Barren-ground Caribou Range.* Canadian Wildlife Service Report no. 21. Ottawa: Canadian Wildlife Service.

―――― 1979. Comments on biologically sensitive areas and biota of Thelon Game Sanctuary. (unpublished)

―――― 1988. Letter to the Honourable Tom McMillan, Environment Canada. (unpublished)

―――― 1988. Thelon should stay just as it is. *Nature Society News* (May: 15).

Lewis, H.F. 1953. *Memorandum on Wolf Control.* Canadian Wildlife Service internal document, (unpublished).

Metcalf, F. 1974. Letters to Ernie Kuyt (unpublished).

Struzik, E. 1989. The Wildlife Bank. *Nature Canada* Spring: 23-28.

Tener, J.S. 1952. *Report of the Musk-oxen Study, Thelon Game Sanctuary, 1952.* Canadian Wildlife Service C.W.S.C. 194, (unpublished).

―――― 1965. *Muskoxen.* Ottawa: Dept. of Northern Affairs & National Resources.

Thomas, D.C. 1988. Letter to Gilles Patenaude, Chairman, Conservation Advisory Committee to the Northern Mineral Policy (unpublished).

Vontobel, R.(ed.) 1987. Government review of Thelon Sanctuary is based on wrong information. *Caribou News* 7(4): 1-2.

Recreational Canoeing

Acheson, K. 1969. *The Canadian Barren Ground: More than a Masochist's Haven* (unpublished).

Cairn Notes. Hanbury-Thelon and Kazan Rivers. (unpublished, forthcoming 1996). Toronto: Betelgeuse Books.

Cramp, F. 1972. *The Hanbury & Thelon Rivers - A Wild Rivers Survey.* Ottawa: National Parks Service.

Finkelstein, M. 1992. *Observations and Explorations along the Thelon River.* Ottawa: Canadian Parks Service.

Greenacre, J. 1983. Hanbury-Thelon. *Nastawgan* 10(1): 8-11.

Hall, A.M. & Voigt, D.R. 1976. Seven Rivers North. *The Beaver* 307(1): 25-33.

Herfindahl, O.C. Across the Barrens by Canoe. *North/Nord.*

Jones, B. 1987. A Rowdy Bunch of Shutterbugs Enlivens a Royal Tour. *The Globe & Mail.* August 7.

Kelly, M.T. 1989. The Land Before Time. *Saturday Night.*

Morse, E.W. 1965. Fresh Water Northwest Passage. *Canadian Geographical Journal* 70(6): 189-96.

———— 1987. *Freshwater Saga: Memoirs of a Lifetime of Wilderness Canoeing in Canada.* Toronto: University of Toronto Press.

Norment, C. 1989. *In the North of our Lives.* Camden,ME: Down East Books.

Olson, D. 1979. Thelon: Flowing with the Ribbon of Life. *Wilderness Camping* Apr/May.

Pelly, D.F. 1990. Down a Wilderness River. *Canoe* 18(3): 14-17,96-98.

Rossbach, G.B. 1966. By Canoe Down the Thelon River. *The Beaver* 297(2): 4-13.

Thompson, D. 1987. Royals in the Barrens. *Che-Mun* 50: 1,3,11.

Thomson S.C. 1989. Down the Thelon: The tundra casts a spell. *Borealis* Fall: 34-38.

Turner, G.M. 1978. Canoe Trip - Hanbury River (unpublished).

Woodley, A.R. 1990. *Thelon River Trip Report.* Yellowknife: N.W.T. Dept. of Economic Development & Tourism (unpublished).

Miscellaneous

Anon. 1953. The Radford and Street Murders. *The Beaver* Sept: 28-29.

Anderson, I.S. 1972. Bathurst Inlet Patrol. *The Beaver* Spring: 20-25.

Bethune, W.C. (ed.) 1934. *Canada's Eastern Arctic: Its History, Resources, Population and Administration.* Ottawa: Canada, Dept. of the Interior.

Berton, P. 1956. Barren Country. *The Mysterious North.* Toronto: McClelland & Stewart.

Choque, C. 1987. *Joseph Buliard: Fisher of Men.* Churchill, Manitoba: R.C. Episcopal Corp.

Clarke, C.H.D. 1978. The Thelon Game Sanctuary. An address with notations to the "Living Explorers of the Arctic" Symposium, Toronto. (unpublished)

Common, R.M. 1978. Letter to Ernie Kuyt from Warden's Grove, Thelon Game Sanctuary, 21 March 1978 (unpublished).

Conservation Advisory Committee on the Northern Mineral Policy 1989. *Thelon Game Sanctuary Report.* Ottawa: Canada, Dept. of Indian Affairs and Northern Development.

Dewar, K.M. 1978. I found the bodies of the Hornby party. *Canadian Geographic* 97(1): 18-23.

Dienger, C. 1990. The Timeless Thelon. *Up Here* Mar/Apr.

Eng, M. et al. 1988. *Known Resource Values of the Thelon Game Sanctuary: A Preliminary Review.* Calgary: The Delta Environmental Management Group.

Hoare, W.H.B. 1930/31. personal journals (unpublished).

———— 1939. Sanctuary. *The Beaver* 270(1): 38-42.

Hodgins, B.W. and Hobbs, M. (eds.) 1985. *Nastawgan: The Canadian North by Canoe & Snowshoe.* Toronto: Betelgeuse Books.

James, W.J.R. 1954. Unpublished essay in Anglican Church Archives, Toronto.

Kerfoot, H. 1978. Geographical Names in the Hanbury and Upper Thelon Area: From Hearne to Cosmos. *Canoma* 4(1):16-23.

MacKinnon, C.S. 1983. A History of the Thelon Game Sanctuary. *Musk-ox* 32:44-61.

Pelly, D.F. and Hanks, C.C. (eds.) 1991. *The Kazan — Journey into an Emerging Land.* Yellowknife: Outcrop.

Raffan, J. 1992. *Frontier, Homeland & Sacred Space: A Collaborative Investigation into Cross-Cultural Perceptions of Place in the Thelon Game Sanctuary, Northwest Territories.* Unpublished PhD thesis, Queen's University.

———— 1993. Where God Began. *Equinox* 71: 44-57.

Struzik, E. 1989. The uncertainty of the Thelon Game Sanctuary. *Above and Beyond* 1(3): 67-72.

Thomson, S.C. 1991. Billy Hoare in the Barrens (unpublished paper delivered to a Wilderness Canoe Association symposium).

Wilson, H.S. 1928. *Report on Prospecting Trip to the Northwest Coast of Hudson Bay via Great Slave Lake and Chesterfield Inlet.* Cobalt, Ontario: Nipissing Mining Co. Ltd.

York, T. 1976. *Snowman.* Toronto: Doubleday Canada Ltd.

———— 1978. *The Musk Ox Passion.* Toronto: Doubleday Canada Ltd.

Index

Choque, Father Charles (1921-) 90

Christian, Edgar (1908-27) 39, 46-57, 73, 127, 128, 134, 135, 143, 154, 159, 168, 172-74

Christian, Marguerite 39, 47

Christopher, William 13, 161

Churchill, Fort 13, 21, 28

Clarke, C.H.D. (1909-81) 61, 98-100, 101, 104, 106, 146, 154, 160, 161

Clarke River 102, 161

Clinton-Colden Lake 16, 165

Common, Robert 167

Cooley, Jim 38

Coppermine (the town) 60

Coppermine River 10, 30, 31

Cosmos Lake 161

Cree 7-10, 11, 123

Critchell-Bullock, James C. 42-45, 55, 59, 157, 159, 162, 172-74

Croft, Clark 37

Crossing-Place-of-Deer 103, 171

Crystal Island 81, 98

Curley, Tagak 147

Dale, Hjalmar 67-69, 71, 159

Damant Lake 122

D'Aoust, Gus (1896-1990) 35-38, 80, 82, 106, 113

D'Aoust, Phil 35

Darrell, Hubert 29

Dene 7, 40, 41, 91, 118, 147-52, 154, 155, 170

Deville Lake 161

Dewar, Ken M. 54, 143, 159

Dickson Canyon 134, 136, 161, 162, 165

Douglas, George 41, 56

Douglas Lake 162

Drybone, Noel 148, 151

Dubawnt River 15, 16, 21, 37, 69, 158

Dunbar, Wayne 132

Ekounelyel 155

Elk River 24, 158

Engle, Bob 136

Ethen-eldili 7, 10, 12, 38, 63, 122-24

Evo, Edwin 147, 148

Eyeberry Lake 162, 185

Fairchild, C.C. 17, 21, 28, 161

Ferguson, Pete 134

Finnie, O.S. 42, 43, 44, 45, 54, 162

Finnie River 100, 104, 162, 170

Fitzgerald, Fort 75, 158

Ford Falls 162

Ford Lake 64

Fort Smith, Pierre 20-21

Fox, Irving 132

French, F.H. 158

French, Pierre 17

Gap, The 148, 164

Goering, Jack 134

Gordon, Bryan 117-25, 141, 167

Grassy Island 102, 112, 115, 148, 160, 162

Great Bear Lake 30, 39, 40, 41, 44, 98, 155

Greathouse, Al 37, 42, 43, 49

Great Slave Lake 12, 15, 16, 20, 25, 28, 29, 31, 32, 33, 34, 36, 40, 41, 42, 48, 53, 62, 70, 77, 83, 98, 133, 136, 158

Gunn, Walter 134

Hall, Alex 131, 137, 138-42, 145, 146, 154

Hanbury, David T. (1864-1910) 13-16, 20, 28-31, 41, 47, 59, 127, 154, 161, 162

Hanbury Lake 136, 162

Harriot, Al 140

Hearne, Samuel (1745-92) 10-12, 21, 30

Helen Falls 44, 102, 109, 127, 128, 130, 131, 132, 137, 162, 165, 167

Herfindahl, Henry 132

Herfindahl, Orris 132, 138

Hill, Tom Hornby 131, 141

Hoare Lake 64, 137, 162

Hoare Point 72, 162

Hoare, W.H.B. "Billy" 54, 55, 60-73, 81, 88, 98-100, 104, 122, 127, 130, 133, 145, 154, 159, 160, 162, 164, 167

Hornby, John (1880-1927) 39-57, 59, 62, 66, 73, 106, 122, 127, 131, 134, 135, 141, 154, 159, 162, 168

Hornby Point 4, 44, 46-57, 67, 100, 103, 119, 133, 135, 141, 162, 165, 168-69

Hudson Bay 7, 10, 12, 13, 15, 28, 29, 31, 32, 43, 55, 85, 127, 158, 160, 161, 182, 184, 185

Hudson's Bay Company 7, 10, 12, 13, 20, 32, 33, 34, 61, 85, 133, 161

Ingstad, Helge (1899-) 37, 38, 42, 47, 67, 68

Inuit 11, 15, 23, 28, 29, 30, 31, 60, 72, 73, 85-93, 105, 109, 121, 124, 125, 133, 147-52, 154, 156, 158, 159, 161, 162, 169, 171